2nd edition

masterMind

Student's Book

Mickey Rogers
Steve Taylore-Knowles
Dorothy E. Zemach

Concept development:
Mariela Gil Vierma

Level 2b

MACMILLAN

Contents

PRONUNCIATION	GRAMMAR	VOCABULARY	LIFESKILLS
SOUNDS: /ʌ/, /ʊ/, and /u/	**REDUCED ADVERB TIME CLAUSES** FUNCTION talking about food labeling and health **REDUCED ADVERB CAUSE–EFFECT CLAUSES** FUNCTION talking about consumption and the environment	**ADJECTIVES ENDING IN *–ABLE/ –IBLE*** FUNCTION talking about sustainable shopping and consumption **MONEY AND FINANCES** FUNCTION talking about personal finance	**WORK & CAREER: EVALUATING CLAIMS** FUNCTION identifying and testing claims
	LANGUAGE WRAP-UP		
WORDS: words ending in *–ical*	**INVERTED CONDITIONALS** FUNCTION talking about hypothetical situations in a formal context **ADJECTIVE PHRASE + INDIRECT QUESTION** FUNCTION talking about non-permanent art	**DESCRIBING ART** FUNCTION talking about meaning and influences in art **NEGATIVE PREFIXES *UN-, NON-, MIS-, IM-, IN-*** FUNCTION talking about opinions on art	**SELF & SOCIETY: DEVELOPING CURIOSITY** FUNCTION learning about the importance of curiosity
	LANGUAGE WRAP-UP		
SOUNDS: assimilation	**THE SUBJUNCTIVE** FUNCTION talking about requests, orders, and recommendations in the workplace **ALTERNATIVES TO THE SUBJUNCTIVE** FUNCTION talking about brain training	**CHILDHOOD DEVELOPMENT** FUNCTION talking about how children learn and develop **MAKING AND RESPONDING TO INVITATIONS** FUNCTION making, accepting, and declining invitations	**WORK & CAREER: RECOGNIZING CONTRADICTION** FUNCTION identifying points in an argument that contradict each other
	LANGUAGE WRAP-UP		
WORDS: thought groups	**INVERSION WITH NEGATIVE EXPRESSIONS** FUNCTION talking about conspiracy theories **ELLIPSIS AND SUBSTITUTION** FUNCTION talking about internet scams	**FALSEHOOD** FUNCTION talking about things that aren't true or real **WORD FORMS (PROVING AND DISPROVING)** FUNCTION talking about proving and disproving claims	**STUDY & LEARNING: EVALUATING INTERNET SOURCE RELIABILITY** FUNCTION checking the reliability of websites
	LANGUAGE WRAP-UP		
SOUNDS: intonation in cleft sentences	**PAST TENSE FOR UNREAL SITUATIONS** FUNCTION talking about hypothetical situations related to music **CLEFT SENTENCES** FUNCTION talking about musicians	**IDIOMATIC EXPRESSIONS WITH *TAKE*** FUNCTION talking about perceptions of famous musicians **SHARING MUSIC** FUNCTION talking about ways of sharing music electronically	**SELF & SOCIETY: IDENTIFYING BIAS** FUNCTION recognizing views that are not balanced or fair
	LANGUAGE WRAP-UP		
SOUNDS: stress shifts in parts of speech	**PARTICIPLE CLAUSES** FUNCTION talking about travel destinations **IMPERSONAL PASSIVE IN THE PAST** FUNCTION talking about natural disasters	**ADVERBIAL MODIFIERS** FUNCTION describing an unusual place **GEOLOGY** FUNCTION talking about geological phenomena	**WORK & CAREER: MAXIMIZING YOUR POTENTIAL** FUNCTION assessing and developing hard and soft skills
	LANGUAGE WRAP-UP		

Irregular verbs & Pronunciation symbols page 176

Grammar review

1 Circle the mistake in each sentence and correct it.

1 My friends would always telling me to go out more. ______
2 Ian is used to speak French. He's lived in Montreal for two years. ______
3 Emma is always get lost on campus. She needs a map. ______
4 I never used drink bottled water until recently. ______
5 My aunt's and uncle's favorite hotel was designed by a rock star. ______

2 Complete the sentences with the modal verbs from the box. You can use some words more than once, and there may be more than one correct answer.

must can't could might may

1 I'm not sure why they aren't here yet. Their car ______ have broken down, I suppose.
2 Did you hear all the people celebrating at the stadium? Their team ______ have won the game.
3 I haven't seen James at work for a few weeks. Do you think he ______ have quit?
4 Where's Patty? She was here a minute ago. She ______ have vanished!
5 Check your missed calls! She ______ have called while you were in a meeting. You never know.

3 Choose the correct verb tense.

1 In the future, people in low-lying countries *may be living* / *are living* in floating houses.
2 Luckily, we *had taken* / *had been taking* several photographs of the view before it clouded over.
3 We hope that by this time next year, a new government *is going to run* / *will be running* the country.
4 By the time Alex arrived, his colleagues *had been discussing* / *had discussed* the proposal for over an hour.
5 Many customers' online accounts *have been* / *are being* hacked recently.

4 Complete the story using the correct form of the verbs in parentheses.

I **(1)** ______ (*have*) an interesting time on my date at the restaurant. We had just finished our main course and Eva **(2)** ______ (*tell*) me about her driving test. Luckily she **(3)** ______ (*pass*), so the small mistake she made when she couldn't turn off the windshield wipers **(4)** ______ (*seem*) pretty funny. Then, in the middle of her story she **(5)** ______ (*stop*) and said she had to leave. I was left alone to pay the bill, and that's when I realized I **(6)** ______ (*leave*) my wallet at home.

5 Rewrite the direct speech as reported speech in two different ways (with and without backshifting) where possible. Use the verbs in parentheses.

1 "I hadn't sent the email when you asked me about it yesterday." (*admit*)
My colleague ______.
2 "Most of the original Native American languages no longer exist." (*declare*)
A researcher ______.
3 "The winner of the *X Factor* has gotten his first number-one hit." (*report*)
MusicReview.com ______.
4 "Usain Bolt will not take part in this year's Indoor Athletic Championships." (*announce*)
Usain Bolt's trainer ______.
5 "I'll send you a text in ten minutes." (*said*)
An hour ago, Nick ______, but he never did.

6 Choose the correct verb form.

1 We regret *informing* / *to inform* you that your application will not be taken further.
2 We tried *liking* / *to like* chili while we were in Mexico, but we just couldn't. It was too spicy!
3 He always complains about *washing* / *to wash* the dishes.
4 Everyone is looking forward to *meeting* / *meet* the new student in the class.
5 Did someone forget *mailing* / *to mail* this letter? Look! It's still on my desk.

7 Complete the sentences with the words from the box. Some can be used more than once.

for so as to so that to

1 Employees should check their emails at the same time every day __________ manage their time better.
2 We joined a social networking site __________ keep in touch with old friends.
3 We booked our tickets well in advance __________ avoid paying a higher price.
4 We are building wells in rural areas __________ local residents can drink safe, clean water.
5 For his birthday, I bought Larry a mug __________ drinking his coffee in the morning.

8 Complete the text using the correct form of *get/be used to* and the verbs in parentheses.

My name's Adriana, and I just left high school and started a job as an air stewardess. I **(1)** *'m not used to working* (*not work*) these kinds of shifts and I find it really difficult to get up at 3 a.m. And I really have to **(2)** __________ (*speak*) English all the time—sometimes I forget and the passengers don't understand me! I **(3)** __________ (*listen*) to English—on TV, for example—but I **(4)** __________ (*not speak*) English outside of school. It's nice earning money, though. I **(5)** __________ (*not pick up*) a paycheck each week—I still get excited about it! The uniform isn't bad. I **(6)** __________ (*wear*) the same thing every day. At least I save money on new clothes.

9 Complete the conditional sentences with the correct form of the verb in parentheses.

1 If you had a sense of humor, you __________ (*see*) the funny side of the joke.
2 I wouldn't try the spicy dishes if I __________ (*be*) you.
3 Some traditions wouldn't have been lost if the languages they belonged to __________ (*survive*).
4 If you __________ (*use*) a firewall, you won't be bombarded with emails from unknown senders.
5 If you change your diet, you __________ (*reduce*) your calorie intake.
6 If you hadn't shopped at the large supermarkets, you __________ (*boost*) the local economy.

10 Rewrite the sentences using the prompts and the words in parentheses.

1 A volunteer succeeded in raising $500 for a charity that helps the homeless. (*manage to*)
A volunteer __________.
2 I'm afraid parents can't park outside the school if they don't have a permit. (*allow*)
Parents are __________.
3 My colleague said, "If I were you, I wouldn't drive to work in these floods." (*warn*)
We were __________.
4 Although Sophie enjoys designing clothes, she doesn't want to organize a fashion show. (*despite*)
Sophie __________.
5 Greater numbers of people are living together before getting married. (*more and more*)
A study reported that __________.

11 Complete the noun clauses with *why*, *what*, *where*, *when*, or *how*.

1 You can see __________ a lot of celebrities don't enjoy the spotlight.
2 I'm not sure __________ that movie is on. Check in the TV listings page.
3 They told me __________ I could attend a meeting about volunteering: at City Hall.
4 Do you know __________ the Hindu calendar celebrates in autumn?
5 Newspapers are learning __________ to adapt to the changing world of technology.

12 In each sentence, two connectors are correct. Cross out the *incorrect* connector.

1 People campaign for causes they believe in. *Besides that, / Despite the fact, / Moreover,* they want to inform and help others.
2 The internet has made communication easier. *Moreover, / Furthermore, / However,* people have learned more about other cultures.
3 Local farmers can stay in business *as a result of / in spite of / due to* people buying their products.
4 Many people do extreme sports *in spite of the fact that / despite / even though* they are aware of the risks involved.
5 This area of coastline was hit by a hurricane last month. *However, / Therefore, / Nevertheless,* few buildings were destroyed.

UNIT 7 THE CRITICAL CONSUMER

IN THIS UNIT YOU

- learn language to talk about the impact of purchasing decisions
- read a magazine article about food labels and what they really show
- talk about money management
- listen to a discussion on sustainable shopping
- write advice for reducing consumption
- learn about evaluating claims
- watch a video about the importance of thinking critically about the food we buy.

READING

understanding explanations and examples

How do examples help you understand a writer's point?

SPEAKING

modifying a statement

Can you think of any times in the last month when you've made a plan and then changed it later, or given an opinion and then changed your mind?

LIFE SKILLS

WORK & CAREER

evaluating claims Do you believe that the statements you see in ads are completely true? Why or why not? Can you give any examples?

A Work in pairs. Look at the pictures and discuss which of the problems in the box, if any, might be associated with each type of food or drink.

health	packaging	pollution	sustainability	transportation

bottled water

fish caught by trawling

organic lettuce

beef from cattle ranching

tropical fruit

B Work in pairs. What kinds of compromises do people sometimes make when they buy food? Discuss some positive and negative aspects of the foods in the pictures.

Bottled water tastes better than tap water, but it's more expensive.

Using bottled water creates more garbage, but it's very convenient.

1 READING: understanding explanations and examples page 63

Explanations and examples are an important type of support for academic texts. They help the reader understand key ideas, and show why a writer's assertion is true or believable. Recognizing these types of support can help with your overall comprehension of a text, and also help you evaluate the strength of its claims.

A Work in groups. Discuss the questions.

1 Do you usually read the labels on packages of food that you buy? Why?
2 Do you think the labels are clear? Are they easily understood? Are they accurate?
3 What kind of information is the most important to have on food packaging?

B Read the text. Decide whether each underlined item introduces an example or an explanation. Which main ideas do the explanations support? What do the examples describe? How do the examples or explanations help you evaluate the strength of the claims?

Interpreting FOOD Labels

5% 0% 1% 3%

1 Packaged foods are required by law to have labels that tell consumers what is in the food. Some consumers, however, may be misled by the language used by food packagers.

2 People tend to think that terms like "light," "low," "reduced," "un-," and "non-" all mean about the same thing, but they don't. (a) Take "sugarless" or "sugar-free"; these terms mean that a product does not contain sugar, although it may contain an artificial sweetener. This is not the same thing as "unsweetened," (b) which means that no sugar or sweeteners have been added.

3 "Fat-free" or "non-fat" means the food contains less than 0.5 g of fat, (c) or fewer than five calories from fat per serving, whereas "light" just means that it has 50% less fat, or 1/3 fewer calories from fat than in the regular version.

4 There are three main things to consider on the label on the back of the package. First, look at the serving size and the number of servings per package. Many people tend to look only at the number of calories, and possibly the amount of fat. (d) The implication of this is that if you don't notice how many servings there are per container and you eat the whole container, you may be eating two or three times the number of calories or amount of fat listed! Quantities listed are based on one serving of the food.

5 The second thing to look at is the list of percentages. These are based on recommended daily intake figures, which are a guideline for how much we should consume every day. They can be maximums for unhealthy things (e) like fats, sugar, and salt, or minimums for healthy things like vitamins, minerals, and fiber. If the maximum recommended amount of sugar is 90 g per day, and a candy bar contains 9 g of sugar, that is 10% of your daily sugar allowance. Check the ratio between healthy and unhealthy things. The label will tell you if a particular food is much higher in fat and sodium than in vitamins, minerals, or fiber. (f) What this means is that this food gives us a lot of "empty calories"; that is, calories with little or no nutritional value.

6 Finally, pay attention to lists of ingredients. Ingredients are listed in order of the amount contained in the food. Watch out for foods with sugar, oil, or sodium at or near the beginning of the list. Some ingredients should be avoided completely, as they have been linked to certain diseases when eaten in large quantities. (g) Examples are aspartame, an artificial sweetener; BHA/BHT, (h) which are preservatives used in oily foods like potato chips; sodium nitrate/nitrite, used as a preservative in processed meats; hydrogenated vegetable oil, which is often used to fry foods; and additives such as artificial food coloring.

C Work in groups. Discuss the questions.

1 What did you learn about food labeling that you didn't already know?
2 Will you read food labels more carefully in the future? Why or why not?

2 GRAMMAR: reduced adverb time clauses

A LANGUAGE IN CONTEXT **Read the survey. What is the general implication of the results?**

Are you a smart food consumer?
Totals for 100 surveyed

		Yes	No
1	Do you make a list before going shopping for food?	40	60
2	Do you take time to read labels while shopping?	30	70
3	When reading a food label, do you understand what all of the ingredients are?	25	75
4	Do you choose a brand only after comparing the ingredients with other brands?	20	80
5	Do you consider serving sizes when eating snack foods?	35	65

B ANALYZE **Read the survey in Exercise A again.**

Form **Choose the correct option to complete the rule. Then complete the table with examples from the survey.**
Clauses that contain adverbs of time such as *before*, *when*, *while*, *since*, and *after* can be reduced (made shorter) when the subject is *the same in both clauses / different in the two clauses.*

NOTICE!

Look at the underlined clauses. In the clauses that don't have stated subjects, circle the verb. Who or what is doing the action?

Rule for reducing the time clause	Full time clause	Reduced time clause
If the clause is in the present progressive, delete the subject and the verb *be*.	Do you take time to read labels while you are shopping?	Do you take time to read labels while **(1)** ________?
If the clause is not in the present progressive, delete the subject and change the verb to the *–ing* form.	Do you make a list before you go shopping for food? When you read a food label, do you understand what all of the ingredients are?	Do you make a list before **(2)** ________ shopping for food? When **(3)** ________ a food label, do you understand what all of the ingredients are?

C PRACTICE **Rewrite the sentences using reduced adverb time clauses.**

1 Leo says he always reads labels when he shops for food.

____

2 I didn't realize how unhealthy diet soft drinks are before I read that article.

____

3 People who eat while they work don't think about serving sizes.

____

4 After she checked the label, Samira decided not to purchase the soup.

____

5 Before it approves a new food, the government agency tests it on animals.

____

6 When they process foods, manufacturers add fat, sugar, and salt to them.

____

WATCH OUT!

✗ While studying, my dog was playing in the yard.

✓ While studying, I watched my dog playing in the yard.

D NOW YOU DO IT **Work in groups. Answer the survey questions in Exercise A individually. Then discuss whether the majority in your group are smart food consumers.**

A: *Well, I think I'm a pretty smart food consumer. I answered "yes" to four of the questions.*
B: *Which one did you answer "no" to?*
A: *Number four. When choosing brands, I never take the time to compare ingredients.*

3 GRAMMAR: reduced adverb cause-effect clauses

A LANGUAGE IN CONTEXT Read the article. How did Annie Leonard come up with the idea for her video?

> **NOTICE!**
> Look at the underlined reduced clauses in the article. Who or what is the understood subject of each one?

The Story of *The Story of Stuff*

While working for Greenpeace, Annie Leonard became interested in the relationship between consumerism and climate change. Having done research on the "life cycle" of consumer products, Leonard decided to make a simple, graphic video that illustrated what happens from the extraction of raw materials to the disposal of a used product. Being convinced that this process is not compatible with the Earth's ecology (most products not being biodegradable), as well as wanting to create something that would be comprehensible to all age groups, Leonard created *The Story of Stuff*. This 20-minute video has had a huge impact, having been viewed millions of times in a number of different languages.

You can watch the video at www.storyofstuff.org.

The Materials Economy

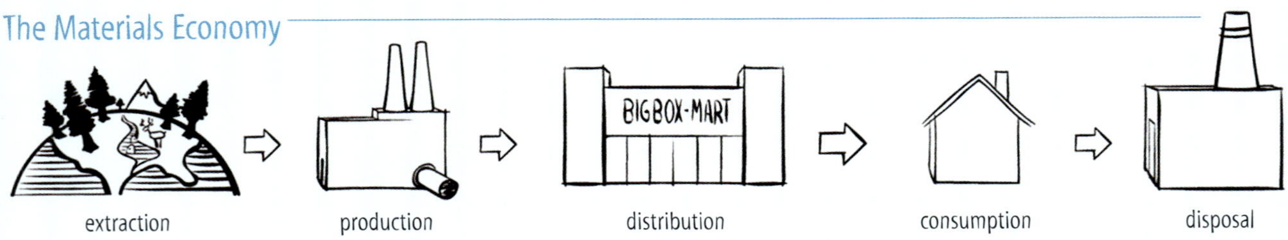

B ANALYZE Read the article in Exercise A again.

Form **Complete the reduced clauses in the table with examples from the article. Then complete the rules with *cause*, *main verb*, or *subject*.**

	Full clause	Reduced clause
1	After/Because she had done research on the "life cycle" of consumer products, …	(1) ________ research on the "life cycle" of consumer products, …
2	(because most products are not biodegradable)	(most products (2) ________ biodegradable)
3	since she wanted to create something that would have an impact …	(3) ________ to create something that would have an impact …
4	since the video has been viewed millions of times, it has had …	has had a huge impact, (4) ________ millions of times …

Rules for reducing the cause-effect clause

- Delete the (1) ________ and the word that signals (2) ________ (e.g., *since*, *because*, *so*).
- Change the verb to the *–ing* form.
- Note that for perfect tense verbs, you change the auxiliary verb (e.g., *have*, *had*), not the (3) ________.

> **WATCH OUT!**
> ✘ Wanting not to see the movie again, we went out for dinner instead.
> ✓ Not wanting to see the movie again, we went out for dinner instead.
> ✓ Not having read the label, I didn't realize there were so many chemicals in it.
> ✓ Having not read the label, I didn't realize there were so many chemicals in it.

C PRACTICE Rewrite the sentences using reduced cause-effect clauses.

1 Since we hadn't seen the video before, we watched it together in class.

____

2 I had read about the video, so I knew what it was about.

____

3 Since most people don't understand the problems with consumption, they don't worry about it.

____

4 Because paper products are recyclable, they are a good option for ecology-minded consumers.

____

5 As some governments are concerned about global warming, they are taking strong action.

____

6 Because they want their students to know about climate change, many teachers use Leonard's video.

____

D NOW YOU DO IT Discuss the questions in groups.

1 Looking at the diagram of the materials economy in the article above, why do you think consumerism affects climate?
2 According to the article and the diagram, is consumption a linear process (going in a straight line, in one direction) or a circular process? Why do you think this might be a problem?
3 In what ways could we reduce the impact of consumerism on the environment?
Having thought about it, I think / want to / am going to … (Not) being a big consumer, I think …

4 LISTENING: to a discussion

A VOCABULARY: ADJECTIVES ENDING IN *–ABLE / –IBLE*

Some adjectives can be made from verbs by adding suffixes. These often have particular meanings. For example *–able* and *–ible* mean "able to be" or "able to."

What are the verb forms of these adjectives? In pairs, try to figure out the meanings. Use a dictionary if necessary.

- accountable
- affordable
- biodegradable
- disposable
- edible
- perishable
- recyclable
- returnable
- reusable

B VOCABULARY: ADJECTIVES ENDING IN *–ABLE / –IBLE* **Complete the sentences with words from Exercise A.**

1 Most glass products are ________________. After being used, the glass can be melted and made into something else.
2 ________________ food will last longer if you keep it in the refrigerator.
3 It's better for the environment to use metal forks and spoons rather than ________________ plastic ones.
4 Companies that do not recycle their waste must be held ________________ for the environmental damage they are causing.
5 Food waste, leaves, and paper are ________________—they are broken down naturally by bacteria.
6 Traveling by bus is more ________________ than going by car because gas is so expensive.
7 Not all wild mushrooms are ________________. In fact, some are quite poisonous!
8 Don't forget to bring ________________ bottles back to the store to get your money back.

C 2.01 **Listen to the conversation. What problems are associated with the products Hans and Caitlin have chosen?**

D **Work in groups. Are the statements on notecard A true for you? Do you agree with the statements on notecard B? Discuss your ideas with your group.**

Notecard A

1 In my family, before buying things like cleaning products, garbage bags, or detergents, we check that the products are biodegradable.
2 We usually bring reusable bags when we go shopping.
3 When shopping for drinks, we look for ones that come in returnable or recyclable containers.
4 We try to avoid using disposable items like plastic plates and cups.

Notecard B

1 In my country, there are a lot of eco-friendly products at affordable prices.
2 When buying perishable items like fruits and vegetables, people often buy too much and then throw out a lot of what they buy.
3 Companies are held accountable for damage to the environment.
4 Stores should only sell drinks in returnable containers.

5 PRONUNCIATION: /ʌ/, /ʊ/, and /u/

A 2.02 **Listen to the lists of words and notice how the vowel sounds are pronounced. Then practice the words.**

/ʌ/ c**u**t, m**o**ney, b**u**dget, imp**u**lse, inc**o**me
/ʊ/ p**u**t, l**oo**k, s**u**gar, sh**ou**ld, w**oo**d, w**oo**l
/u/ f**oo**d, tr**ue**, s**oo**n, f**oo**lish, s**u**per, cons**u**me

B 2.03 **Work in pairs. Listen to the sentences, paying special attention to the vowel sounds practiced in Exercise A. Then practice the sentences with your partner.**

1 I buy food on impulse in the supermarket.
2 It's foolish to spend money on goods that you don't need.
3 You should start budgeting your money soon.
4 Food is biodegradable, as are natural materials like wood and wool.
5 Putting less sugar in your coffee is an easy way to cut down the number of calories you consume.

6 SPEAKING: modifying a statement

In the course of a discussion, we often decide to modify or completely change something we have said. We use signaling phrases to let our listeners know that we are going to do this.

A 2.04 **Listen to the conversation. What is Alex's problem? What do his friends advise him to do?**

B Listen again. Then check the phrases that mean that the speakers are going to modify something they said.

☐ I know.
☐ That said, …
☐ Well, …
☐ But then again, …
☐ Although actually, …
☐ … having thought about it, I …
☐ On second thought, …
☐ … having said that, I …

C VOCABULARY: MONEY AND FINANCES The verbs on the left are all from the conversation in Exercise A. Match them with the words on the right to form collocations.

1	to be	a)	a budget, a plan, a list
2	to stretch	b)	your income, money
3	to buy something	c)	impulse buying, expenses
4	to be able to	d)	on impulse, on sale, on credit
5	to stick to	e)	broke
6	to cut down on	f)	afford something, pay your bills

D VOCABULARY: MONEY AND FINANCES Check the best answer for you for each statement in the survey. Then compare with a partner.

		Always true	Sometimes true	Seldom true
1	I look for ways to stretch my money.	☐	☐	☐
2	I'm broke at the end of each month.	☐	☐	☐
3	I don't buy things on impulse.	☐	☐	☐
4	I make shopping lists and stick to them.	☐	☐	☐
5	I am able to follow a budget.	☐	☐	☐
6	I try to cut down on my expenses when I can.	☐	☐	☐
7	I try to buy things on sale when I can.	☐	☐	☐
8	I can never afford to do or buy anything extra.	☐	☐	☐

E Work in groups. Discuss your answers to the survey in Exercise D. Do you think you are a good money manager? Why or why not? Remember to use phrases to modify your statements when necessary.

HOW TO SAY IT

I think I'm a fairly good money manager because I ..., although actually, / but then again, ...

I always think I'm a disaster/not that great with money. But having said that, / thought about it, I ...

7 WRITING: offering advice

A Work with a partner. Brainstorm a list of everything that you think you absolutely have to buy over the course of one year. Compare your list with another pair.

B Read the blog post. Which piece of advice would be easiest for you to follow? Which would be hardest?

The Year of Nothing New

It's been a crazy year! But we made it—well, mostly. As you know, if you've been following this blog, we couldn't always live up to our goal of "Buy nothing new this year." But I think we came pretty close. I'll write another more in-depth post on what we learned about ourselves through this experience, but I wanted to share here some of our tips for avoiding buying things. You're probably not as crazy as we are, and you're going to buy some stuff. But everyone should probably cut down on buying. Remember—our planet belongs to everyone, and we have to take care of it. We're all accountable.

- *Reduce your media consumption.* Seriously—the more you see, the more you want to buy. Having turned off our TV service for a year, we weren't watching all those ads. After installing ad blockers on our internet browsers, we didn't see new products pushed at us all the time. And if we didn't know it was available, we didn't buy it.
- *Don't go into stores without a plan.* How many times have you walked out of a store with items that were on sale, or a new color, or just because they caught your eye, having gone into the store just to buy one or two things? Resist impulse buying by making a list before you go of what you're going to buy. And then stick to it!
- *Wear things out.* Use your stuff till it breaks, falls apart, or is too old to be practical. Printers, phones, computers, refrigerators, cars—you don't need a new one every two years. Wear your clothes until they have holes, not just until the next fashion magazine comes out. Stretch the life of your stuff, and you'll stretch your budget too.
- *Buy things that last.* Don't be tempted by non-rechargeable batteries, plastic forks, paper cups, single-use cleaning wipes. It doesn't matter if they're recyclable because it still leaves a carbon footprint to manufacture them and transport them.
- *Find happiness from non-material things.* The most important part of "reduce, reuse, recycle" is reduce. Reduce the amount of things you buy. Instead, give your spirits a lift by taking a walk in the park, hanging out with friends and talking, playing a musical instrument, or singing a song—you're limited only by your imagination!

C Work in pairs. Write two or three more pieces of advice for reducing consumption. Write them as bullet points, as in the article above. Include details to explain how to do each thing and why it is effective.

D Post your advice on the classroom wall. Read all of the advice. Decide which ones could work best for you. Then discuss your ideas with your partner.

lifeSkills

EVALUATING CLAIMS

- Identify the claims made.
- Think of questions to test the validity of the claims.
- Do research to check the validity of the factual claims.

A Work in groups. Read the two ads and discuss the questions.

1 Would you buy either of these two products? Why or why not?
2 What is the purpose of
   - the pictures in the ads?
   - the colors?
   - the design?
   - the type of language used?

B Work in groups. Study the ads more carefully and complete the table. Then discuss how the factual claims could be proved or disproved.

	Sugar-free gum	Milk
Claims		
Questions about the claims		

C Read the information about the two products. Then discuss the questions in groups.

1 Which of the claims in the ads were supported by the information in the article?
2 Was there any information that contradicted claims made in the ads?
3 Having read the information in this text, have you changed your opinion about whether to buy either product? Why or why not?

ADVERTISING CLAIMS—TRUTH OR FICTION?

[1]The FDA (Food and Drug Administration) is cracking down on unsupported claims by food manufacturers. A number of food companies have been told to change or eliminate claims of health benefits on their packaging and in their ads. Some of the biggest violators of FDA regulations are cereal and snack-food companies.

[2]A number of products are also being targeted by consumer groups and medical organizations. One controversial product is sugar-free gum. Manufacturers claim that sugarless gum promotes dental health, helps with weight management, aids in concentration, and helps reduce stress. Research shows that chewing sugarless gum does, in fact, help promote dental health through stimulation of saliva production. Saliva helps wash away harmful acids, and it contains calcium, which helps strengthen tooth enamel. However, claims that chewing gum helps with weight management, concentration, and stress reduction are not so well-documented, and there is no indication of how much gum you have to chew to obtain these effects. Finally, all gum contains chemical dyes, flavorings, and preservatives, which some scientists believe are not good for your health.

[3]Another product getting attention from medical researchers is milk. Milk producers make several claims that are disputed by a number of doctors. First, they claim that the calcium in milk promotes bone growth and helps prevent osteoporosis, a bone disease. In fact, one study published in the *American Journal of Epidemiology* showed that people who had consumed dairy products in their 20s were more likely to suffer hip fractures when they were older. The second claim is that teenagers should drink four cups of milk every day. The doctors say that four cups of whole milk contain 33 grams of fat, of which 20 are saturated fat, and that drinking that much milk can contribute to the problem of teenage obesity, so teenagers should be sure to drink low-fat milk. Finally, milk companies say that everyone, not just kids, should drink more milk. This ignores the fact that many adults are lactose intolerant: it's thought that about 15% of Caucasian-Americans, 70% of African-Americans, 50% of Mexican-Americans, and 90% of Asian-Americans fall into this category.

HOW TO SAY IT

Having analyzed these ads, we've realized/decided/learned …

We think that when reading ads, people should …

After reading the article, we've concluded that …

REFLECT … How can the skill of evaluating claims be useful to you in **Self & Society** and **Study & Learning**?

RESEARCH …

Find an ad that makes claims about what a product does or what benefits it has. You can check websites, magazines, newspapers, television, or radio ads. Make a list of the claims. Identify whether they are factual claims or opinion. Describe how the factual claims could be checked. If possible, check the factual claims yourself. Do they seem to be true? Why or why not?

Language wrap-up

1 VOCABULARY

Complete the text with ten of the words and phrases from the box. (10 points)

accountable afford affordable biodegradable broke cut down on disposable on impulse perishable recyclable returnable stick to stretch

Be a Smart Consumer

Having spent most of my young adult years being **(1)** __________, I learned to be a pretty careful consumer. Maybe some of the things I learned to do can help other people both **(2)** __________ their money and reduce their carbon footprint. First, make yourself **(3)** __________ for everything you buy—if you buy it, write it down! Second, make a shopping list and **(4)** __________ it. Don't buy lots of things **(5)** __________, and don't buy things you're not really able to **(6)** __________. If you **(7)** __________ unnecessary purchases, you'll not only save money but you'll reduce clutter in your home. When grocery shopping, buy only small amounts of **(8)** __________ items, so you don't waste food. Finally, buy things like beverages in **(9)** __________ rather than **(10)** __________ containers. You'll get a deposit back when you bring the containers back, and it's also better for the environment.

8–10 correct: I can use adjectives ending in *–able* and *–ible* and words related to money and finances.
0–7 correct: Look again at Sections 4 and 6 on pages 85 and 86. SCORE: /10

2 GRAMMAR

Check the correct sentences. Then rewrite the incorrect sentences, using a correct reduced clause where possible. (10 points)

1 After doing a lot of reading on advertising, I feel that I know much more about it. ☐

2 After made a list of everything I bought last week, I looked at what I could cut down on. ☐

3 Didn't kept a record of my purchases, I really didn't know how much I was spending. ☐

4 While shopping for food, my brother ran into an old high school friend. ☐

5 While driving to the store, a truck ran into my car. ☐

6 Not want to be too critical, I didn't question the doctor's recommendations. ☐

7 We were sure that the meat wasn't good, we didn't buy it. ☐

8 Having a lot of problems with money in the past, I now keep a list of my expenses. ☐

9 Not wanting to spend much money, we bought only a few things that we really needed. ☐

10 Before buy food in a package, be sure to read the label. ☐

8–10 correct: I can use reduced adverb clauses of time and cause-effect.
0–7 correct: Look again at Sections 2 and 3 on pages 83 and 84. SCORE: /10

WRITING WORKSHOP

Interpreting charts

A Read the assignment and a student's response. What change to the city's recycling program would the writer recommend?

The chart gives information about the volume of recycled materials in a particular year. Summarize the information by selecting and reporting the main features. Interpret the information and draw conclusions and/or make recommendations.

[1]The chart shows what types of material were recycled. The amount of each material is indicated as a percentage of the total materials recycled. Slightly more than half of all recycled material is paper. This could be because paper is very widely used and one of the easiest materials to recycle. Most offices and schools have collection containers for paper recycling, and curbside residential recycling collects newspapers, mail, and other household paper goods.

[2]The fact that residential recycling is popular can be seen from the next largest category, yard trimmings, which accounts for slightly less than a quarter of all recycled material. Yard trimmings include grass, leaves, and bits of plants and trees that are biodegradable. The city collects these materials directly from residences for a small fee. Larger pieces of wood, however, must be taken by the resident to a special recycling area, which is probably the primary reason the recycling rate for wood, although it is also biodegradable, is so low—less than 3%.

[3]Metal, glass, and plastic make up about 10% of recycled materials. This figure could increase if recycling these materials were easier. People must separate plastic, glass, and metal into different containers. Additionally, only some types of plastic can be recycled. Cities where residents can mix plastic, metal, and glass into one container show significantly higher recycling rates for these materials.

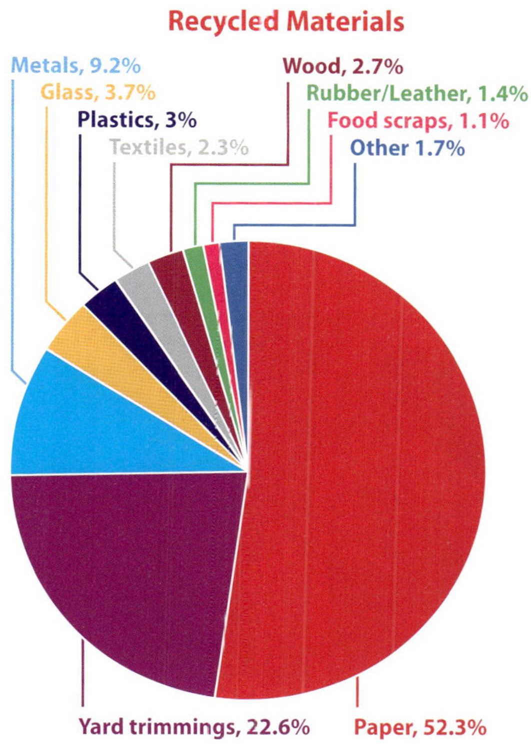

B Read the response again. In pairs, answer the questions.

1 Underline the sentences that *describe* figures given in the chart. How is the information expressed differently from the chart?
2 Double underline the sentences that *interpret* the figures in the chart or provide additional information that is not in the chart. Do you think the conclusions or recommendations are based on information in the chart or the student's own knowledge?

C Prepare to write a summary of what people in Springfield throw away. Study the chart and make notes to help plan your summary.

1 What are the two largest categories?
2 What could be the reasons for this?
3 How might people be able to reduce what they throw away in the most significant categories?
4 How might this chart change in the future?

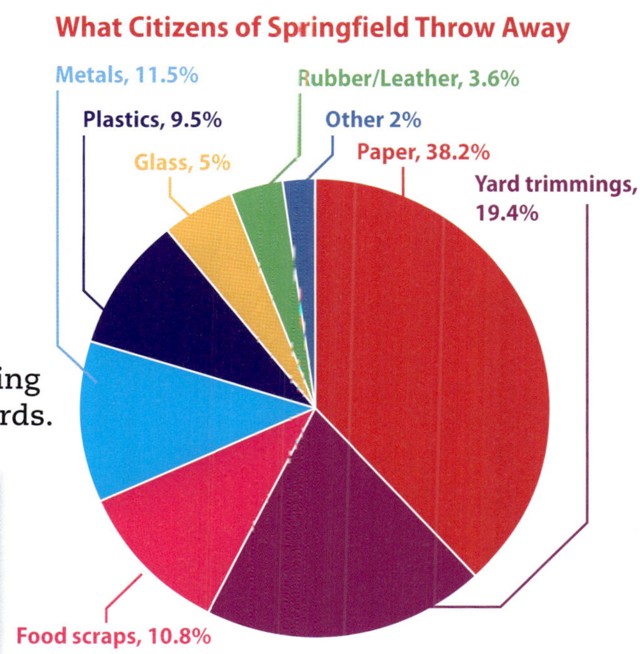

D Summarize the information in the chart by selecting and reporting the main features. Write about 250 words.

HOW ARE YOU DOING?

- ◯ I summarized the most important information.
- ◯ I interpreted the information.
- ◯ I offered my opinions about what the information means.

UNIT 8 ARTISTIC LICENSE

IN THIS UNIT YOU

- learn language to talk about art
- listen to a lecture about the Surrealist school of art
- write a review of an event
- read about some influential graffiti artists
- talk about meaning in art
- learn about the importance of curiosity
- watch a video about a piece of public art

LISTENING
inferring factual information

Why do you think some speakers don't state every idea directly?

WRITING
a review

Do you usually read reviews before you buy a product, go to a restaurant, visit a place, or go to an event? How do reviews help people?

Jean Luc Cornec TribuT (1995–2014) © DACS 2014

LIFE SKILLS
SELF

developing curiosity Do you like to ask questions when you encounter new situations, circumstances, or people? Why might it be useful to do so?

A Rank the art from 1 (= your favorite) to 6 (= your least favorite).

B Work with a partner. Share and explain your rankings. Then take turns describing what each piece of art looks like.

1 LISTENING: inferring factual information page 73

When we infer information, we make guesses or form opinions based on the information we already have. Speakers often expect the listener to infer certain information or to draw conclusions. Pay attention not only to the words you hear, but also to what those words suggest or imply.

A As a class, look at the paintings on this page. Talk about what you know or think about Surrealism and Surrealist artists.

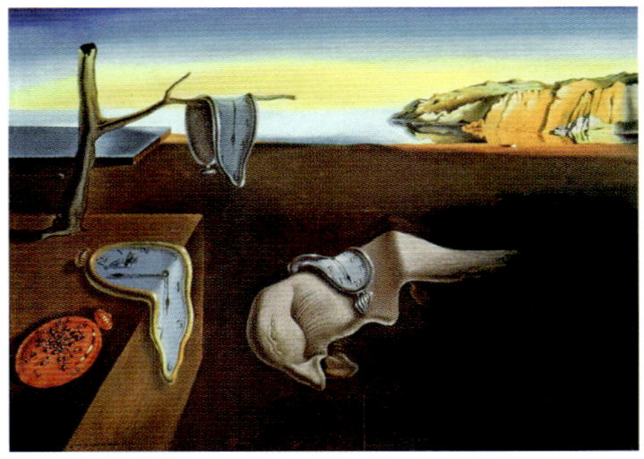

The Persistence of Memory, Salvador Dalí, 1934

Syssigy, Leonora Carrington, 1957

B 2.05 Read the quiz before you listen to the lecture. As you listen, take notes if you want to. Then choose the best answer for each item.

1 The Surrealists … influenced by the effects of World Wars I and II.
  a) were b) were not
2 Surrealism places a lot of importance on …
  a) everyday objects.
  b) dreams.
  c) both.
3 The professor thinks that Salvador Dalí's work … serious art.
  a) was b) was not
4 The professor considers Leonora Carrington to be an important representative of Surrealism in …
  a) Britain.
  b) the U.S.A.
  c) Latin America.
5 There … many female painters at the time the Surrealist movement started.
  a) were b) were not

C Listen again. Then work in pairs. Compare your answers and say what information helped you to infer each answer.

D VOCABULARY: DESCRIBING ART Complete the definitions with the words from the box.

concept controversial illustration proportion represent school symbol unconventional

1 ________ topics or people cause strong opinions for and against them.
2 A/An ________ is an idea of something that exists.
3 To ________ something is to stand for something or to mean something.
4 A/An ________ is one thing that stands for or is used to mean another thing.
5 If objects in a painting are in ________, this means they are the right size or shape compared to other objects around them.
6 A/An ________ is an example used to show that something is true, to show what something is like.
7 ________ people, ideas, or things are different from what most people consider to be usual or normal.
8 A group of writers or artists whose work or ideas are similar is called a/an ________.

E VOCABULARY: DESCRIBING ART Work in pairs. Discuss what you think the paintings on this page mean. How are they typical of the Surrealist genre? Use as many words from Exercise D as you can.

2 GRAMMAR: inverted conditionals

A LANGUAGE IN CONTEXT Read the biography of a famous American artist. What influenced Louis to change his style?

NOTICE!

Read the underlined phrases. What is unusual about the word order? Are the sentences questions?

Morris Louis (1912–1962) was an American painter of the Washington Color school. When he moved to Washington, D.C., to teach art, he became a friend of the painter Kenneth Nolan. Had he not met Nolan then, he might never have developed the abstract style for which he is known today. Unfortunately, his painting style was also what caused his death. Paints at that time contained many toxic materials, and breathing paint fumes could cause cancer. Had Louis worked in a larger room, or with different materials, he probably wouldn't have contracted the lung cancer that killed him.

Now that these health risks are known, modern painters can learn something from the sad case of Louis. Should you choose to work with toxic materials, work in a large, well-ventilated space and take frequent breaks. Better yet, select paints and other art supplies that don't create toxic fumes.

B ANALYZE Read the biography in Exercise A again.

Form Complete the sentences in the table with examples from the biography.

	Standard conditional	Inverted conditional
Present	If you choose to work with toxic materials, work in a large, well-ventilated space.	(1) ________ you ________ to work with toxic materials, work in a large, well-ventilated space.
Past	If he hadn't met Nolan at this period, he might never have developed the abstract style for which he is known today.	(2) ________ he ________ Nolan then, he might never have developed the abstract style for which he is known today.
	If Louis had worked in a larger room, he probably wouldn't have contracted the lung cancer that killed him in 1962.	(3) ________ Louis ________ in a larger room, he probably wouldn't have contracted the lung cancer that killed him in 1962.

Function Choose the correct option to complete each rule.

1 Inverted conditionals are more *formal* / *informal* than standard conditionals.
2 Inverted conditionals are more common in *writing* / *conversations*.

WATCH OUT!

✗ Hadn't he met Nolan then …
✓ Had he not met Nolan then …

C PRACTICE Rewrite the sentences as inverted conditionals.

1 If Claude Monet hadn't been nearsighted, he might not have painted objects as soft and blurry.

____

2 If you paint with colors such as cadmium red or cobalt blue, wear gloves to protect your skin.

____

3 If she had known how dangerous the paint fumes were, she would have used a fan.

____

4 If you melt metal or glass with a blowtorch, always wear protective goggles.

____

D NOW YOU DO IT Work in pairs. Make sentences about these ideas. Use inverted conditionals. Then share your sentences with another pair.

- something you would like to warn people not to do now
- something you would like to advise people to do now

3 PRONUNCIATION: words ending in *–ical*

A 2.06 Listen to the pairs of words. Which ones undergo a stress shift? How many syllables do those words have?

logic logical
critic critical
practice practical
biography biographical
history historical
politics political

B 2.07 Listen to the sentences, paying attention to the words from Exercise A. Then practice the sentences with a partner.

1 The 1920s was a critical period in American art history.
2 I read a fascinating historical biography of an art critic.
3 That's not a very practical policy, even if it seems logical.
4 Political movements are often represented in art, as you can see from this biographical article on the Surrealists.

4 SPEAKING: talking about meaning in art

A Look at the painting and read the description. Do you think this is what the artist wanted to express in the painting? Can you think of any other ways to explain its meaning?

B 2.08 Listen to a conversation about the description in Exercise A. What are the man's objections?

C VOCABULARY: NEGATIVE PREFIXES: *UN-*, *NON-*, *MIS-*, *IM-*, *IN-* **Write the negative forms of the adjectives in the box in the correct columns of the table.**

Maturity, **Trinh Tuan, 2008**

Trinh Tuan works with unconventional, non-standard materials, and contrasts form and color in an unusual way. In this work, the viewer gets an immediate sense of the loneliness and alienation of a couple who are unloving and mismatched. Though they are touching, the strong black line between them symbolizes an invisible, immovable wall that they are unable or unwilling to cross.

able comprehensible controversial interesting interpreted
loving movable original standard understood visible willing

un-	non-	mis-	im-	in-
unconventional	non-traditional	mismatched	impossible	insufficient
unusual				

D VOCABULARY: NEGATIVE PREFIXES: *UN-*, *NON-*, *MIS-*, *IM-*, *IN-* **Look back at the painting in Exercise A. Use the questions to help you form an opinion of it.**

1 Is this painting original and interesting? Why or why not?
2 Is the theme of the painting easily interpreted by the average viewer? Why or why not?
3 Do you agree more with the interpretation in Exercise A, or with the man in Exercise B? Why?
4 Do you like the painting? Why or why not?

E Independent Speaking Work in pairs. Give your opinion of the painting. Use as many words from Exercise C as you can.

5 GRAMMAR: adjective phrase + indirect question

A 2.09 **LANGUAGE IN CONTEXT** **Listen to the conversation. What do the speakers think about the meaning of non-permanent art?**

Emily: These ice sculptures are amazing! I'd love to know how they do it.

Josh: Yeah, I'd love to try it myself! It would be good to find out whether they use special tools. I bet it takes a long time, though!

Jane: I know! It's hard to understand why people go to all that trouble to create non-permanent art!

Emily: Well, it's interesting to think about what the non-permanent aspect really means. I mean, maybe it doesn't mean anything, or maybe it's a kind of commentary on our modern world.

Jane: I don't know. I think it's natural for people to wonder what the deeper meaning of everything is, but it's impossible for me to see where the deep meaning is in something that will be a pool of water in a few days!

NOTICE!

Find and underline the question words (e.g., *what*, *how*) in the text. Are they being used in direct questions?

B **ANALYZE** **Read the conversation in Exercise A again.**

Form **Complete the table with examples from the conversation.**

It + be	adjective	(*for* + indirect object)	infinitive	indirect question (e.g., *what/when*)
(1) ________	(2) ________	–	to find out	whether they use special tools.
It's	hard	–	to understand	(3) ________
It's	interesting	–	to think about	(4) ________
(5) ________	(6) ________	(7) ________	to wonder	(8) ________
It's	impossible	for me	(9) ________	(10) ________

Function **Choose the correct options to complete the rules.**

We use **adjective phrase + indirect question** to talk about a question being considered, usually when a definite answer is (1) *known* / *not known*. We (2) *expect* / *don't expect* an answer to this question. We use (3) *it is* / *it would be* with verbs like *find out* or *know when* we talk about an action we might take in the future.

WATCH OUT!

✗ It would be good to find out could I take a course in ice sculpting.

✓ It would be good to find out if/whether I could take a course in ice sculpting.

C **PRACTICE** **Rewrite the direct questions as indirect questions using the words and phrases in parentheses.**

1 Where do they have sand sculpture exhibits? (*interesting / find out*)

____

2 Is there any non-permanent art in our community? (*nice / know*)

____

3 Why is non-permanent art so popular? (*easy / see*)

____

4 Have there always been forms of non-permanent art? (*difficult / know*)

____

5 What does abstract art symbolize? (*hard / me / understand*)

____

6 What was the world like when abstract art began? (*important / us / consider*)

____

D **NOW YOU DO IT** **Work in groups. What do you know about other types of non-permanent art? What would you like to know?**

6 READING: an article about art

A Work in pairs. Discuss the questions.

1 Is there much graffiti in your community? Where do you usually see it? Who do you think creates it?
2 What do you think inspires graffiti artists? Where do they get their ideas?
3 Do you think graffiti artists should be paid for their art?

B Read the article. What are some similarities between Haring and LADY PINK? What are some differences?

The Art of GRAFFITI

[1]Graffiti commonly refers to writings or drawings that have been placed in public spaces such as the sides of buildings without permission and in secret. Topics commonly include comments on social or political topics, stylistic portrayals of the artist's name (known as "tagging"), or simple drawings.

[2]When we think of graffiti, we invariably think of unwanted scrawls on the walls of businesses or names spray-painted onto the sides of buses or trains. In most areas, painting someone else's property without permission is considered vandalism, which is a crime. However, had these laws been strictly enforced, the world would have missed some great art—and some great artists such as these:

KEITH HARING

[3]Born in 1958, Haring's first art influences were the cartoon images of Dr. Seuss and Walt Disney. Haring attended a commercial art school in Pittsburgh, but soon dropped out, realizing he actually had little interest in commercial art. Instead, he moved to New York to attend the School of Visual Art. It was an important move in many ways: had he not relocated, he might not have met the musicians and artists, including graffiti artist Jean-Michel Basquiat, who inspired both his spirit and his work. Haring found graffiti to be creative, spontaneous, and provocative—all qualities he admired.

[4]In 1980, Haring found a unique outlet for his creative impulses: unused spaces for ads in the New York City subway system, covered with black paper. Haring used white chalk to cover these large surfaces with the simple line drawings that became his signature style. He created hundreds of these drawings in the early 1980s, sometimes completing 30 or more drawings in a single day.

[5]Of course, it was impossible to remain invisible while drawing in such public spaces, and Haring drew much attention. In fact, he noted, his subway drawings were performances as much as art. And people were intrigued by his images. "I was always totally amazed that the people I would meet while I was doing them were really, really concerned with what they meant. The first thing anyone asked me, no matter how old, no matter who they were, was what does it mean?"

[6]His style was clear and recognizable, and many residents of New York knew Haring's art before they knew his name.

LADY PINK

[7]LADY PINK was born in 1964 in Ambato, Ecuador, as Sandra Fabara. At the age of seven, she moved to New York City.

[8]When she was 15 and still a student at the High School of Art and Design, Fabara's boyfriend was arrested and sent home to Puerto Rico. As a reaction to this, Fabara began tagging neighborhood walls with his name. Soon she began tagging walls with her own name—or rather with her new name LADY PINK.

[9]She joined a few different graffiti crews of other artists, mainly painting subway trains. The impermanence of street art didn't bother her. "Graffiti artists learn not to get attached to their work," she said in an interview with the Huffington Post. "When you put up a public work, whether it's on a subway car or the wall of a building, you kiss it goodbye." She became well-known as one of the only working female graffiti artists and started exhibiting her work in galleries. In 1982, at age 18, she starred in the film Wild Style, and she had her first solo show when she was just 21. For a while in the late 1980s, she stopped painting outdoors, but returned after marrying graffiti artist Smith. The two now work together to produce commercial artwork. LADY PINK's art has been exhibited in museums such as the Metropolitan Museum of Art in New York and the Groninger in Holland.

C Work with another pair. Discuss the questions.

1 Why do you think the artists chose to create art in public spaces where it might be removed? Do you think their art would have the same effect if viewed in a gallery?
2 Should graffiti artists get permission before painting in public spaces? What about private property?

7 WRITING: a review

Good reviews, whether of a product, service, or event, usually have a similar structure. When you write a review, include an introduction to give basic information on what you are reviewing. Then clearly state what you liked and/or did not like, and why. Finally, say whether or not you would recommend the item or event.

A Read the review and answer the questions.

1 What kind of information does the writer give in the first paragraph?
2 What is the purpose of the next two paragraphs?
3 What two things does the last paragraph do?
4 How might the structure of the review be different if the writer recommended the event?

B Read the review again. As a class, discuss how the writer follows the outline format, and what details are given about each point.

Artifacto

EVERYONE'S TALKING ABOUT …

JULY 1–31st GOLDEN GATE PARK

THE AMATEUR ARTISTS' FAIR

1 The Amateur Artists' Fair is a large art fair sponsored by the City of San Francisco at Golden Gate Park, and admission is free. The fair is open every weekend this month.

2 There were several things that I liked about the fair. First, the exhibitors are in specific sections according to their type of art. There's a sculpture section, a painting section, a jewelry section, and so on, which makes it easy to see and compare all the exhibits in each genre. The entertainment was also enjoyable. There were workshops where children could make art of their own, and for adults, there were several good local live bands.

3 There were, however, a number of problems with the fair. First, there was insufficient parking, so we had to park really far away. Second, the fair was so crowded that it was hard to see some of the exhibits. Furthermore, people were allowed to bring their dogs, which is incomprehensible to me. I'm not talking about guide dogs, but people's pets—which their owners seemed unwilling or unable to control. Finally, in my opinion, the exhibits were uneven in terms of quality. There were a few very good artists there, but a lot of the art was really not very good. I would also have liked to see more controversial themes that challenged viewers to think, as well as unconventional styles, instead of picture after picture of trees and roses. It would be interesting to know how they chose the exhibitors.

4 Although an amateur art fair is a very good idea, it's essential for the organizers to consider how many people will attend an event like this and plan for that number. It's also important for them to decide what level of quality they want in the exhibits and accept only exhibitors who show that quality in their work. Finally, I would like to see them seek out art that has something to say, that offers a fresh look at something, or that makes a statement worth considering. In conclusion, I would be unwilling to recommend the Amateur Artists' Fair to anyone who is hoping to discover innovative, challenging, or high-quality works from new artists.

C Think of an event you have attended and make notes for a review in your notebook. Remember to think about the structure you will use.

D Write your review. Assume that the event is still going on, and say whether you recommend it.

E Work in pairs. Exchange reviews. Read your partner's work and say whether the review is logically structured.

lifeSkills

DEVELOPING CURIOSITY

- Understand the value of curiosity.
- Develop curiosity-building techniques such as careful observation and asking questions.
- Apply these techniques to new situations.

A **Work in groups. Discuss the questions.**

1 Curiosity is a common trait shared by most people in the arts. How do you think this attribute influences their art? In what other professions do you think curiosity is a common trait?

2 In English, there are two meanings of the word *curious*. How could this sentence be interpreted? *He is a very curious man.*

3 The phrase *curiosity killed the cat* is commonly used in English. What do you think it means?

4 One of the most frequent words used by young children is *why*? How do adults often react to this, in your experience?

B **Work with your group from Exercise A. Read the first section of the article and discuss the two statements. Then read the second section and discuss why curiosity can be referred to as a life skill.**

Psychology Monthly—August Edition

Did Curiosity Really Kill the Cat?

Stop and think for a moment about the relationship between these two factual statements. What challenge do they present?

FACT Studies have shown that children's curiosity and creativity drop when they enter kindergarten; they drop further around the fourth grade, and still further in the seventh grade.

FACT 21st century employers are putting increasing emphasis on hiring people with creative thinking and innovation skills.

Parents (and teachers, and employers), take note: curiosity should be rewarded, not stifled.

Have you ever noticed that successful people tend to be very good at a number of different things? It's not necessarily true that these people are more gifted than other people. What is true is that they are probably intensely curious. They want to learn new things, and learning something new develops our abilities to think, to adapt, and to solve problems. Curiosity is a natural human trait, though different people possess the trait to different degrees. It is probably safe to say that curiosity played a role in the survival and development of the human species by helping to make the human brain the agile, problem-solving organ it is today. Curiosity makes the mind active rather than passive, and an active mind is a strong mind. Curiosity also makes us observe and anticipate new ideas, and it leads us to discover new possibilities and ways of doing things. This, of course, leads to advancements in our societies. Finally, curiosity brings excitement to our lives. It gives our lives variety and stimulus, and these things make us happy. A society, a workplace, or a family that encourages curiosity is dynamic, innovative, and healthy.

C Take the quiz to find out how curious you are—your "curiosity quotient" (CQ).

A Curious Quiz

Before you start the quiz, think about how you would answer this question: Do you consider yourself to be a curious person?

		Yes	Somewhat	No
1	I'm constantly asking questions.			
2	I notice details about people and places.			
3	I think learning is fun.			
4	I like doing new or non-routine things.			
5	I like reading or talking about almost anything.			
6	I like talking to people who have different opinions from mine.			
7	I often find that something I once thought was boring is interesting.			

Add up your score and find out your CQ. Does this change your previous opinion about how curious you are?

Scoring: Yes = 2, Somewhat = 1, No = 0
10–14: Very curious, **4–9:** Moderately curious, **0–3:** Not very curious

D Work in groups. Try these curiosity-building activities.

Activity 1: Observe. Pay attention to details in your surroundings.

- Walk around and observe the room you are in. Don't talk, but do use as many of your senses as possible.
- Come back to your group and say what you noticed that you had never noticed before, or what you noticed about the other people in the room.

Activity 2: Ask questions with the words *why* and *how*.

- Take a few minutes to brainstorm things you would like to know, to answer questions with How or Why. For example, "Why do we yawn when we are tired?" or "How do fish sleep?"
- Write two or three questions beginning with "It would be interesting/fun to know how/why …"
- Discuss your questions with your group.
- Remember that the first part of being curious is questioning, but the second part is being curious enough to find out the answer. Decide who in your group is going to find out the answer to each unanswered question. Then go and find out.

E As a class, brainstorm as many reasons as you can why curiosity is an important trait.

REFLECT … How can the skill of developing curiosity be useful to you in **Work & Career** and **Study & Learning**?

RESEARCH …

Search for sayings and quotations about curiosity. Look for both original English sayings and for those translated from other languages. Prepare a short presentation for your class on what the sayings or quotations literally mean and what attitude toward curiosity they show.

Language wrap-up

1 VOCABULARY

Read the paragraph and choose the correct options to complete the text. (10 points)

Many people find abstract art to be **(1)** *incomprehensible / uncontroversial* because it doesn't look realistic. They say an art form that does not show people or objects is easily **(2)** *unmovable / misinterpreted*. The **(3)** *concept / school* of abstract painters included Jackson Pollock, Mark Rothko, Willem de Kooning, and many others, who claimed that "paint is paint, and canvas is canvas, and they should not pretend to be otherwise." Abstract art uses line, color, shape, and **(4)** *proportion / concepts* to convey a mood or feeling. One **(5)** *illustration / school* of this is the paintings of Piet Mondrian. All signs of the natural world seem **(6)** *unoriginal / invisible* at first, but if you understand that, for example, Mondrian used vertical lines as **(7)** *symbols / schools* of manmade buildings and towers, and that horizontal lines **(8)** *interpret / represent* landscapes, the works begin to make sense.
Even if you are **(9)** *unable / unloving* to understand abstract paintings completely, you can still enjoy them. They might be difficult to understand, but they are unusual and creative—and certainly not **(10)** *unwilling / unoriginal*!

8–10 correct: I can describe art and use negative prefixes to form opposite adjectives.
0–7 correct: Look again at Sections 1 and 4 on pages 94 and 96. **SCORE:** /10

2 GRAMMAR

A Put the words in the correct order to form sentences. (5 points)

1 people to / it's / describe what / modern art / hard for many / means / .

____

2 to know / was carved / this statue / when / it's impossible / .

____

3 for / how much / it's difficult / a painting / me to guess / costs / .

____

4 why I want / an artist / to understand / my parents / it's hard / to be / for / .

____

5 this sculpture / it / what / be nice / represents / to figure out / would / .

____

B Complete the sentences with the correct form of the inverted conditional. (5 points)

1 ______________ (*you / read*) *The Moon and Sixpence* by Somerset Maugham, you will discover that it is based on the life of French painter Paul Gauguin.
2 ______________ (*he / be famous*) while he was alive, Gauguin might not have been so poor.
3 ______________ (*he / not / study*) Gauguin's work, Pablo Picasso might have painted differently himself.
4 Had Gauguin not found Paris too conventional, he ______________ (*might / not / move*) to Tahiti.
5 ______________ (*you / visit*) Tahiti, you can see a fine collection of Gauguin's works, including sketches, paintings, and sculptures.

8–10 correct: I can use inverted conditionals and adjective phrases with indirect questions.
0–7 correct: Look again at Sections 2 and 5 on pages 95 and 97. **SCORE:** /10

SPEAKING WORKSHOP

Proposing a solution

A 2.10 **Listen to a student's proposed solutions for problems caused by pigeons in cities. List the solutions. Which one does the speaker prefer?**

1 ______
2 ______
3 ______

B Listen again. Check the phrases for talking about problems and solutions that you hear.

- ☐ … it's important to …
- ☐ … in several ways …
- ☐ There are two main ways in which this is a problem.
- ☐ Three solutions … have been proposed.
- ☐ The first is that …
- ☐ Another way to address the problem is to …
- ☐ … is a better idea …
- ☐ … would not be effective because
- ☐ The best of these solutions is …
- ☐ … would be the smartest solution.

C In pairs, brainstorm possible solutions to the problem in the box. Then individually, choose the three best solutions.

Local business owners are complaining about graffiti on the sides of their buildings. They say the graffiti is unattractive, and it costs a lot of money to remove.

D Prepare and practice a presentation about proposed solutions to the problem of unwanted urban graffiti. Include at least two solutions. Explain which one you think is the best and why.

HOW ARE YOU DOING?

- ◯ I explained the problem clearly.
- ◯ I explained which solution I thought was best.
- ◯ I ordered the solutions by putting the best one last.

UNIT 9 JUST PLAYING?

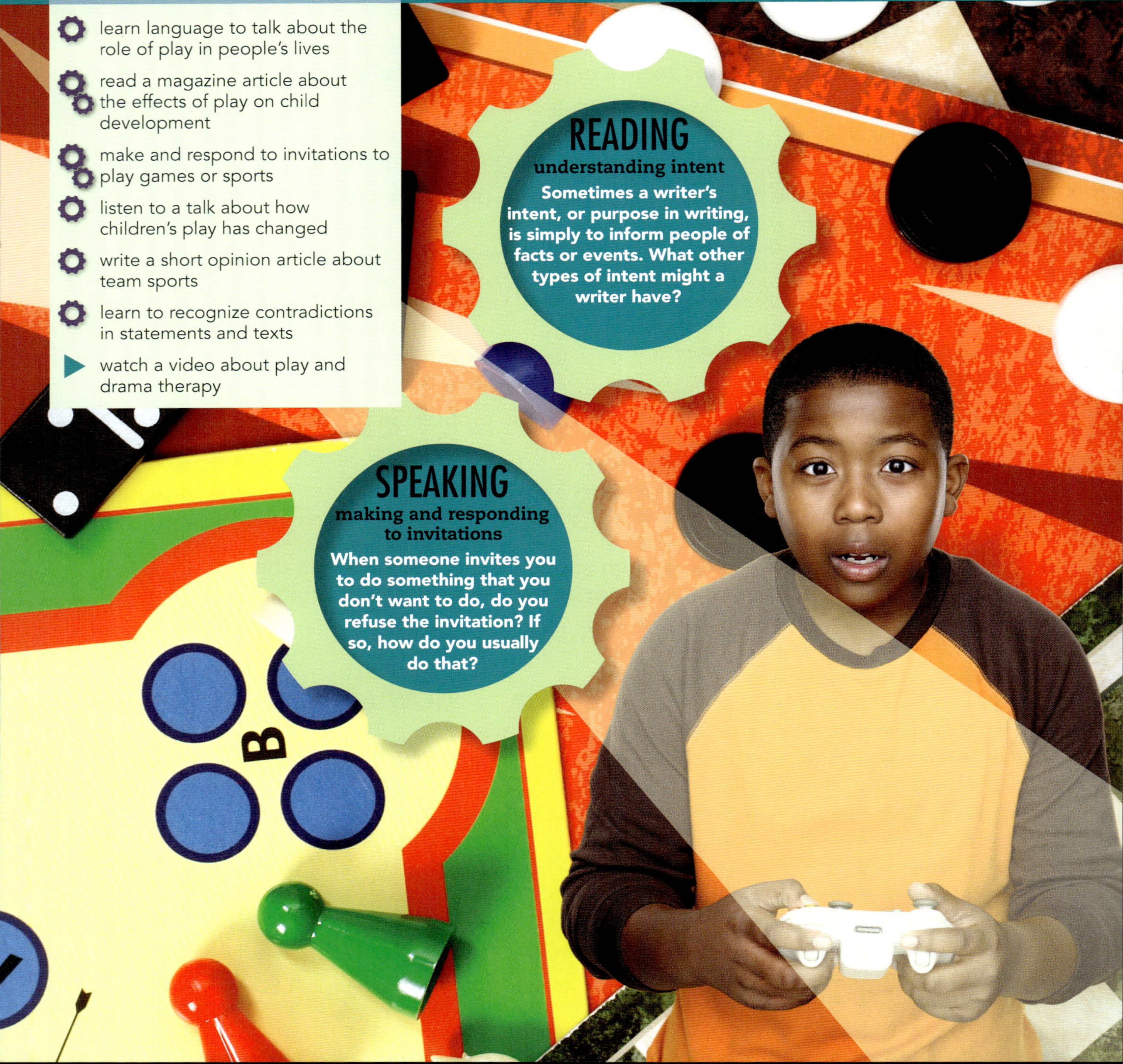

IN THIS UNIT YOU

- learn language to talk about the role of play in people's lives
- read a magazine article about the effects of play on child development
- make and respond to invitations to play games or sports
- listen to a talk about how children's play has changed
- write a short opinion article about team sports
- learn to recognize contradictions in statements and texts
- watch a video about play and drama therapy

READING

understanding intent

Sometimes a writer's intent, or purpose in writing, is simply to inform people of facts or events. What other types of intent might a writer have?

SPEAKING

making and responding to invitations

When someone invites you to do something that you don't want to do, do you refuse the invitation? If so, how do you usually do that?

LIFE SKILLS

WORK

recognizing contradiction Why is it important to be able to recognize points or statements in an argument that contradict each other?

A As a class, discuss which of the following statements express your attitude toward play.

"Adults have lots of different forms of entertainment, of course, but only children really play."

"Everyone should play an organized sport. Playing sports is good for us—physically and mentally."

"Toys and games should be educational so that children learn while they're playing."

"Childhood is a time when you should play as much as possible—there's plenty of time for work when you're older."

B Work in groups. Discuss the questions.

How do children play? How do adults play? What do you think children and adults gain from playing? Consider these areas and use the pictures to help you think of ideas:

- physical skills
- social skills
- experience
- knowledge

1 READING: understanding intent

Every text is written for a particular purpose. It might be to entertain, to inform, to persuade, or it might have a combination of different aims. By establishing the writer's intent—the aim or purpose—you may understand the text better, and you'll be able to evaluate whether the writer has achieved his/her purpose.

A Discuss the questions as a class.

1 Do you think the amount of time today's children spend playing is the same as when you were a child? If not, do you think children play more or less now?

2 Do children play differently now than when you were a child? If so, what are some of the differences?

B Read the article. Does the writer seem generally optimistic or pessimistic about current developments in children's play? Why is that?

The Vital Role of PLAY in Early Childhood Education

By Joan Almon

[1]In over 30 years of working with young children, I have observed one consistent feature of childhood: creative play is a central activity in the lives of healthy children. Play helps children weave together all the elements of life as they experience it. It is an **outlet** for their creativity, and it is an absolutely critical part of their childhood. The unique qualities of each child become apparent in the way they play. Some cultural differences **emerge**, for children **imitate** what they see around them. But there are strong universal qualities in play. For example, three-year-olds around the world play in similar ways; their play is different from that of five- or six-year-olds.

[2]Studies show strong relationships between a child's capacity to play and his or her overall development—physical, social, emotional, and intellectual. Despite its central importance in children's healthy development, play is now seriously endangered. Children have become dependent on electronic entertainment: television, DVDs, tablets, smartphones, and video games. When media-filled children do play, their games are naturally full of media characters and stories. It becomes increasingly hard for children to make up their own creative stories in play.

[3]Kindergarten programs focus so strongly on teaching **literacy** and **numeracy** that many children no longer have time to play. In a typical six-hour day at a public kindergarten, children spend 90 minutes on early literacy drills, 60 minutes on mathematics, and 30 minutes on science. They have about 30 minutes for outdoor play. Three- and four-year-olds are now expected to **engage in** far more early writing and reading activities than ever before.

[4]Given the importance of play for children's physical, social, emotional, and mental development, the demise of play will certainly have serious consequences. Indeed, there is growing concern about what kind of society we are creating if a generation of children grows up without play and the creative thinking that emerges from it.

[5]If imaginative free play continues to disappear from childhood, I anticipate several serious **outcomes**, including difficulties in the way children socialize and communicate with each other, more aggression in social relationships, and a loss of creative thinking. If one does not develop curiosity and **open-ended** thinking, how does one approach today's social, political, economic, and ecological problems? I am very concerned that without opportunities for open-ended, imaginative play, our children will not be capable of this type of creative thinking as they grow older.

[6]Nation after nation is rushing toward removing play from young children's lives in the misguided belief that three- to six-year-olds are ready for direct instruction in early literacy and other academic topics. For the sake of the children, and for the sake of the society they are part of, this direction needs to be reversed now and play needs to be restored as an essential part of childhood.

Joan Almon–iaswece.org

C Match each paragraph of the article (1–6) with its purpose (a–f).

Paragraph 1	a) makes an appeal for action
Paragraph 2	b) refers to research
Paragraph 3	c) states a concern
Paragraph 4	d) refers to personal experience
Paragraph 5	e) quotes statistics
Paragraph 6	f) explains the concern

D Work in pairs. Choose the statement that best summarizes the writer's overall intent. Then explain how each of the paragraphs helps the writer express that intent.

The writer's intent is to …

a) compare how children play now with how they played in the past.
b) inform the reader about the role of play in different age groups.
c) persuade the reader that we need to encourage creative play for children.

Paragraph 1 helps the writer achieve her purpose by telling the reader that she knows what she's talking about because she's been working with children for over 30 years.

E VOCABULARY: CHILDHOOD DEVELOPMENT Write the words and phrases in bold from the article in Exercise A next to the correct definitions.

1 ________________ (*n.*): results
2 ________________ (*v.*): appear; become known
3 ________________ (*n.*): a way to express ideas
4 ________________ (*n.*): basic skills in math
5 ________________ (*v.*): do, take part in
6 ________________ (*v.*): copy someone's behavior
7 ________________ (*adj.*): not restricted
8 ________________ (*n.*): the ability to read

F VOCABULARY: CHILDHOOD DEVELOPMENT Work in groups. Do you agree or disagree with the statements? Give reasons.

1 You're never too young to improve your literacy and numeracy.
2 When children fight, it's a natural outlet for their feelings. It doesn't mean that there are larger problems.
3 Imitating adults is an excellent way for children to learn appropriate behavior.
4 Because kids don't engage in much open-ended play anymore, people are becoming less creative.
5 Games can often produce better learning outcomes than more structured types of teaching.

2 LISTENING: to a radio talk show

A Look at the pictures. Which one most resembles your own childhood?

B 2.11 Listen to the beginning of a radio show. Check the two main points the speaker makes.

Barbara, 64:

☐ I understand why the way children play has changed.
☐ Play has become more interesting than it used to be.
☐ Children used to engage in more imaginative play.
☐ Children today get bored less easily than in the past.

C 2.12 Now listen to the rest of the radio show. For each person, note down examples of how they think play has changed.

Becky, 38:

____

____

____

Pedro, 25:

____

____

____

D Work in pairs. Compare your notes. Say which of the points you think are true and why.

3 GRAMMAR: the subjunctive

A LANGUAGE IN CONTEXT Read the paragraph. Why does Jeff's company encourage employees to play at work?

NOTICE!

Circle the verbs that come after ***that***. What form are they in? What verbs or adjectives come immediately before ***that***?

ALL WORK AND NO PLAY? NOT IN OUR OFFICE!

Jeff is a software designer at a small software company. He is playing table tennis at work, but that's not a problem because his company insists that he spend part of his work day playing! His boss asks that he take a break every couple of hours to do something fun. Many psychologists now recommend that people spend more time playing and less time working. They say it is essential that people relax and have fun in order to be more productive. They also say it is important that a person not work too many hours without taking a break. Also, it is recommended that everyone play a sport or game during at least some of those breaks. Of course, most companies don't *demand* that their employees take time off to play. Some simply suggest that workers not spend the whole day at their desk. Some final advice from Jeff, though: "Just don't spend too long playing and forget to work. It definitely isn't recommended that you play *all* the time!"

B ANALYZE Read the paragraph in Exercise A again.

Form Write the underlined sentences in the paragraph in the correct places in the table.

Use	Form	Examples
With verbs: *ask, demand, insist, propose, recommend, suggest, require*	**Affirmative:** subject + verb + *that* + subject + base form	(1) ______________
	Negative: a) subject + negative verb + *that* + subject + base form	(2) ______________
	b) subject + verb + *that* + subject + *not* + base form	(3) ______________
With adjectives: *recommended, necessary, essential, better/best, important*	**Affirmative:** *It* + *be* + adjective + *that* + subject + base form	(4) ______________
	Negative: a) *It* + *be* + *not* + adjective + *that* + subject + base form	(5) ______________
	b) *It* + *be* + adjective + *that* + subject + *not* + base form	(6) ______________

Function Choose *T* (true) or *F* (false) for the rules.

1 The subjunctive is used in formal English to emphasize requests, orders, and recommendations. *T / F*
2 With both verbs and adjectives, the two negative forms have exactly the same meaning. *T / F*

C PRACTICE Choose the correct verb form to complete each sentence.

1 It was necessary that he *check / checked* the figures several times.
2 It *is / be* essential that you arrive on time.
3 They asked that we *not take / don't take* a break.
4 It was recommended that they *allow / allows* us to play at work!
5 Parents demand that all school games *be / are* educational.
6 My boss asked me *work / to work* ten hours yesterday!
7 They recommended that employees *not work / didn't work* on Saturdays.
8 It is essential that we *be / are* there tomorrow.

WATCH OUT!

✘ Her manager recommended that she takes a break.
✓ Her manager recommended that she take a break.

D NOW YOU DO IT Work in pairs. Discuss how a company can increase employee motivation, and how employees can improve their work environment.

It is essential that a company pay workers a fair salary.
Employees should demand that the company provide recreation areas.

4 SPEAKING: making and responding to invitations

There are certain phrases we use to make and respond to formal and informal invitations. We often use short phrases and informal language to make or decline informal invitations, but we use complete sentences and very polite language for formal invitations.

A 2.13 Listen to three conversations and check the correct boxes.

	Formal	Informal	Accepted	Declined
Invitation 1				
Invitation 2			Paul:	Paul:
			Olivia:	Olivia:
Invitation 3				

B VOCABULARY: MAKING AND RESPONDING TO INVITATIONS
Listen again. Then complete the phrases in the table.

Making an invitation	Accepting an invitation	Declining an invitation
Informal (1) You __________ it? (2) __________ go?	Informal (5) __________!	Informal (7) __________ do tonight. I have to … (8) __________ a rain check? (9) __________ later …?
Formal (3) __________ you to … (4) __________ to …?	Formal (6) Yes, I __________ to …	Formal (10) I'd really like to go, but unfortunately, I __________.

C VOCABULARY: MAKING AND RESPONDING TO INVITATIONS
Work in pairs. Role-play the situations. When you have finished, switch roles. Use phrases from the table in Exercise B.

Student A:
Student B is in one of your classes, and you know him/her well. Start a conversation with Student B and invite him/her to join you in an activity that you are planning for this evening. If your invitation is declined, try to persuade the person.

Student B:
Student A is in one of your classes, and you know him/her well. Student A will invite you to do something this evening. Politely decline the invitation, using appropriate phrases.

Student A:
You are Student B's boss or professor. Invite him/her to go to a talk on an interesting topic. If he/she accepts, explain the arrangements to go there.

Student B:
Your boss or professor is inviting you to go and hear a talk. Politely accept the invitation and make arrangements to go there.

5 GRAMMAR: alternatives to the subjunctive

A LANGUAGE IN CONTEXT Read the paragraph. Do you find the results of the studies surprising? Why or why not?

NOTICE!

Find and underline the verbs and adjectives that are normally followed by a verb in the subjunctive form. Are all of those verbs followed by subjunctives in this text?

Researchers Recommend Training Your Brain Through Play!

The fast pace of life demands that your brain function at its top capacity. Some researchers recommend increasing brain function by playing video games of the type that require you to think and react very quickly. Some studies have found that people who do best at video games are able to process visual information more quickly than people who don't play regularly. Of course, spending too long in front of a screen can have negative effects on your health, so you should limit the time you spend playing, especially if your job requires sitting in front of a computer screen for hours. Furthermore, it's important for you to include games that are specifically designed to increase brain function. So, are you up for a game?

B ANALYZE Read the paragraph in Exercise A again.

Form Complete the table with examples from the paragraph.

Use	Alternative form	Example
With verbs *insist, demand (that)*	(No alternative: subjunctive only)	*His parents insisted that he play only educational games.* (1) ______
With verbs *ask, require*	verb + object + infinitive	*The rules require you to choose five words.* (2) ______
With verbs *require, recommend, suggest, propose*	verb + gerund	*I suggested measuring the effects of brain training games.* (3) ______ (4) ______
With adjectives *important, essential, vital, necessary, good/better/best*	*It* (+ *would*) + *be* + adjective (+ *for* + object) + infinitive	*It would be better for him to stop playing video games.* (5) ______

Function Choose the correct option to complete the rule.
The alternatives to the subjunctive in the table above have *the same meaning as / a different meaning from* the subjunctive.

WATCH OUT!

✗ He suggested to learn a sport.
✓ He suggested that I learn a sport.
✓ He suggested learning a sport.

C PRACTICE Rewrite the sentences with alternatives to the subjunctive.

1 It is vital that we exercise our brains as well as our bodies.
______
2 The company recommends that employees learn to play at least one video game.
______
3 It is essential that you keep your brain active.
______
4 I propose that our company give the employees free video games.
______
5 Our boss is asking that we attend a brain training workshop.
______

D NOW YOU DO IT Work in pairs. Discuss the question.

- What can employers do to help employees maximize their brain power?

6 PRONUNCIATION: assimilation

A 2.14 **Listen to the words and phrases. Notice the sounds of the final consonants in a word or a syllable before the /j/ sound.**

Final consonant sounds /s/, /z/, /t/, /d/, + /j/ = new consonant sound

/s/ + /j/ = /ʃ/	/z/ + /j/ = /ʒ/	/t/ + /j/ = /tʃ/	/d/ + /j/ = /dʒ/
issue	pleasure	nature	procedure
this year	does your	that your	would you

B 2.15 **Listen to the sentences. Then practice saying them with a partner. Pay attention to the underlined consonant combinations.**

1 The issue is that your membership in the games club expires this year.
2 Is your mental capacity a function of nature or nurture?
3 Would you prefer to play a game just for pleasure or one that lets you increase your mental functions?

7 WRITING: a short article

A **Read the announcement from a magazine. What kind of article are the editors of the magazine looking for?**

Here at *Young Perspectives*, we're always trying to find ways to question conventional attitudes and opinions. We don't want to hear the same old opinions—it's important for us to challenge and question them. That's why each month we ask our readers to send us short articles on controversial subjects. Here is this month's winning article: "Video Games: Why They're Good for You!" Look out for next month's topic and get thinking, get writing, and send us an article!

B **Read the winning article. Then choose T (true) or F (false) below.**

Video Games: Why They're Good for You!

[1]I have to admit that I've wasted many long hours playing video games—and felt guilty about it afterwards! Surely I should have been using my time more effectively, doing something productive? Well, in fact, rather than beating myself up about it, it turns out I should be congratulating myself. I wish I'd known sooner that I had actually found one of the best ways to improve my brain power and to socialize better! What's more, I had fun doing it!

[2]We all know the horror stories. Teenagers get fat and lazy and ruin their brains playing meaningless video games. They do worse in school the longer they spend on games. It's essential for us to stop kids from playing so many video games, etc., etc. What they never tell you is how playing those games develops so many of your skills. First of all, many games involve real-world skills, like planning ahead, or consulting maps. Playing these games requires you to stretch your mental abilities in all kinds of ways.

[3]Apart from that, games these days are social affairs. Most of them can be played with other people over the internet. It's important for gamers to engage in lots of interaction with their teammates and plan their strategy together. They console each other for failures and compliment each other on successes. In other words, they use and develop their social skills. In fact, with many online games, the players who do the best are those who cooperate well with other players.

[4]It's vital that we all stop feeling guilty about the time we spend playing games and proudly announce the truth: Playing video games is good for you! Want to join me for a game?

1 The writer uses a formal style. T / F
2 The writer refers to his/her own experience to personalize the text. T / F
3 The writer uses humor to engage the reader. T / F

C **Write a 200–300 word article for *Young Perspectives* about next month's topic: Should everyone play a team sport at some point in his/her life? Decide which side of the argument you support, choose a title for the article, and write the article.**

lifeSkills

RECOGNIZING CONTRADICTION

- Learn to recognize points that contradict each other. If two points cannot both be true, then they are contradictory.
- When you hear or read an argument, try to identify the main idea and the main points. Then decide whether any of the points contradict each other.
- Decide whether an argument is strong or weak based on how many contradictory points there are.

A Read the statements about play. Match each statement (1–4) with another statement (a–d) that directly contradicts it.

1 Rather than wasting time playing, young children should focus on activities that develop numeracy and literacy. ___
2 Children learn about the adult world by imitating it in play. ___
3 Children socialize better when they are left without adult supervision. ___
4 Children should use play to explore the limits of their physical world. ___

a) Playing is often a distraction from the business of learning to live in the real world.
b) The most important thing is to keep children physically safe.
c) Play can help children develop a number of academic skills that they need to learn.
d) It's best for parents to organize their children's free time to avoid fights or other problems.

B Work in pairs. What is the contradiction in each quote? Underline the relevant sentences.

"My daughter spends about an hour each day playing video games and at least an hour playing outside with friends. I make sure she plays properly and doesn't just waste time. I think play is an important part of children's lives because it helps their mental and social development. They learn to make their own decisions, and they learn how to socialize with other children. Play is an essential part of childhood in my opinion."

"I didn't like traditional games when I was a kid, and I spent most of my time playing computer and video games. A lot of people say that those games have negative effects on kids, but they haven't affected me. The games taught me a lot of skills, like following maps or planning ahead. They also taught me about technology, and I work with computers now. The only problem I can see is that children can become pretty isolated playing those games. I know that as an adult, I'm a little uncomfortable in social gatherings, and I prefer to do things on my own, but I'm good at my job."

C Read the assignment and the extract from a student's essay. What are the three main points the writer makes?

Under the title *The Dangers of Gaming*, give your opinion on the possible negative consequences of spending too much time playing video games.

The Dangers of Gaming

[1]Since video games became a part of everyday life in the 1980s and 90s, there has been controversy over their possible negative effects. Parents, politicians, and the media have all expressed concern about the way they influence young people. While some of this may be dismissed as hysteria and panic, there is no doubt that some real dangers connected to gaming have emerged.

[2]One of the most serious consequences of gaming is addiction. The symptoms of game addiction can be similar to the symptoms of drug addiction. An increasing number of young people sit in one spot playing games for hours each day, often losing weight and withdrawing from the outside world. They may suffer from disrupted sleep, seem anxious when prevented from playing, and lie about the amount of time they spend on games. In some countries, young people are sent to special clinics to cure them of their addiction even though there is no real evidence that it is actually a physical or psychological condition.

[3]Even in those who don't become addicted, anti-social behavior is a common effect of gaming. Gamers these days often play games that take place online and that involve interacting with a wide range of people. They may spend less time with their real-world family and friends. This can lead to a variety of problems at home, at school, or at work as friends and colleagues start to feel rejected.

[4]Too much time spent on video games also leaves less time for other activities. People who play games extensively do not get the chance to develop other sides of their character which require interacting meaningfully with other people, such as the ability to empathize. Spending too much time in the narrow worlds that games create means you develop a narrow view of the world, without an understanding of the wider context in which we all live.

D Read the essay again. The writer makes two statements that contradict other points made in the essay. Find and underline them.

E Work in pairs. Compare your ideas from Exercise D. Decide how you would edit the text to correct the contradictions.

F Work in groups. Do you agree with the writer's argument? Why or why not?

G Discuss the questions.

1 When you read an argument, do you usually question what you read and look for contradictions? If you notice contradictions, does this make you question the validity of the whole article?
2 How can following the suggestions in this lesson help you think about arguments more critically?

REFLECT ... How can the skill of recognizing contradictions be useful to you in the areas of **Self & Society** and **Study & Learning**?

RESEARCH ...

Choose a controversial topic that you are interested in. Find blogs, editorials, or other types of written opinions on the topic and analyze the arguments. Tell the class about one or two of the arguments you found and whether you found any contradictions.

Language wrap-up

1 VOCABULARY

A Complete the paragraph with the words from the box. (5 points)

engage in   imitate   open-ended   outcomes   outlet

Often in the past, children were expected to be seen and not heard. Teachers might have seen play as a useful **(1)** ________________ for excess energy, but they probably felt it was not as important as the development of academic skills. Over time, even the strictest adults began to see that play had a wider function and could lead to a number of positive **(2)** ________________. Children learn many skills when they are allowed to **(3)** ________________ free, **(4)** ________________ types of play such as inventing stories or games. They also learn from older children and adults, as we can see when they **(5)** ________________ actions and behaviors they see in real life.

B Complete the conversations with the words from the box. (5 points)

a rain check   sorry   sounds great   up for   want to

1 **A:** Are you **(1)** ________________ going out tonight?
B: Sorry. Can I take **(2)** ________________? I have to study.

2 **A:** Hey, **(3)** ________________ go out with me and a few friends for dinner?
B: That **(4)** ________________! What time?

3 **A:** Would you like to attend the regional conference next week?
B: Oh, I'm **(5)** ________________, but I can't. I'll be out of town.

8–10 correct: I can talk about childhood development and make and respond to invitations.
0–7 correct: Look again at Sections 1 and 4 on pages 106, 107, and 109. **SCORE:** /10

2 GRAMMAR

Choose the correct options to complete the letter to a school principal. (10 points)

Dear Ms. Claiborne,

We are writing because of some concern over recreation policies at the school. Everyone agrees that it **(1)** *be / is* important for children **(2)** *play / to play*, both at school and at home. However, it is also essential that educators and parents **(3)** *don't / not* allow young children to play completely unsupervised, and we have heard that this is your approach. You have said that it's better **(4)** *let / to let* kids play on their own so that they learn to resolve problems for themselves. We feel that children need adult guidance to learn to do this, and we propose **(5)** *to have / having* at least one teacher present at all times while the children are playing. We ask that the teacher **(6)** *help / helps* the kids resolve any differences before they become serious. We are not demanding **(7)** *for / that* the teacher **(8)** *interrupt / interrupts* small arguments, but we do want to insist that teachers **(9)** *give / will give* a bit more guidance to our children. We propose not **(10)** *let / letting* this matter wait until the next official meeting. Could we have a short meeting with you next week?

Very truly yours,

Forest Hill Parents' Association

8–10 correct: I can use the subjunctive and alternatives to it.
0–7 correct: Look again at Sections 3 and 5 on pages 108 and 110. **SCORE:** /10

WRITING WORKSHOP

Writing a short article

A Read the assignment and the response. Then choose T (true) or F (false) for the statements below.

Assignment: Choose a type of game or sport that you think helps people develop mental, physical, or social skills, or a combination of skills. Write an article of about 250 words explaining why you think this is true.

Dominoes: More Than a Game

[1]We hear a lot about the advantages and disadvantages of playing organized sports and of playing video games. However, we very rarely hear about the effects of playing other types of games such as cards, board games, or dominoes. In my opinion, dominoes is a game that has many advantages and no disadvantages.

[2]Here is why dominoes is much more than just a game, and why it is definitely not a waste of time. First, playing dominoes is a social activity. It is possible to play dominoes online, but I think it's important that people play this game face to face with friends or family. It's a lot more fun that way, and players develop skills like patience (sometimes people take forever to make a move!) and good sportsmanship (you can't always win!). Second, dominoes helps people develop numeracy skills. You learn to add numbers quickly in your head, and you learn to make educated guesses about what dominoes the other player probably has. Finally, playing dominoes requires you to develop analytical skills. You have to try figure out what your opponent will do, and you have to create strategies. In order to win, it's important not to simply react to the other player's moves; you should have a strategy that allows you to plan several moves in advance.

[3]In conclusion, playing dominoes requires thinking and planning, so it is a good way to train your brain. Best of all, it's fun and it doesn't cost money to play!

1 The writer lists three main benefits of playing dominoes. T / F
2 The writer says that people who are not good at math will not be able to play dominoes. T / F
3 According to the article, dominoes helps people develop a variety of skills. T / F
4 The writer thinks that playing dominoes can help improve mental functions. T / F

B Read the article again and complete the outline.

Paragraph 1: Introduction
Hear a lot about advantages of video games and sports
Other types of games never mentioned
Topic sentence: ________________

Paragraph 2: Advantages of dominoes
Topic sentence: ________________
Is a social activity
Develops numeracy skills
Also develops ________________

Paragraph 3: Conclusion
Topic sentence: ________________
Also fun and ________________

C Read the assignment in Exercise A again. Prepare an outline similar to the one in Exercise B about a different game or sport. The topic sentence of each paragraph should state the main idea.

D Use the outline to write your article. Write about 250 words.

HOW ARE YOU DOING?

- ◯ The first paragraph introduces my opinion.
- ◯ There is a topic sentence in each paragraph which states the main idea of the paragraph.
- ◯ I have given several reasons to support my opinion.

UNIT 10 FACT OR FICTION

IN THIS UNIT YOU

- learn language to talk about popular beliefs and falsehood
- listen to a conversation about ideas on social networking sites
- write a wiki article about a popular belief
- read about a website that checks popular beliefs
- talk about popular beliefs
- learn about checking the reliability of internet sources
- watch a video about people telling personal truths and lies

LISTENING

difficult situations

When someone speaks very quickly and you find it difficult to understand, what can you do about the situation?

WRITING

a wiki entry

Have you ever edited something someone else has written, or written something with someone else? What are some possible problems in these activities?

LIFE SKILLS

STUDY & LEARNING

evaluating internet source reliability

Do you think information on the internet is generally reliable? Does it depend on the website? Explain your opinion.

A Work in pairs. Look at each of the pictures and check whether you think they show something real or fake. Explain.

giant coconut crab real ☐ fake ☐

world's smallest cat real ☐ fake ☐

UFO real ☐ fake ☐

scorpions on sticks real ☐ fake ☐

rabbit-shaped fruit real ☐ fake ☐

hole in the sidewalk real ☐ fake ☐

B Work in small groups. Discuss whether you agree or disagree with the statements.

"People will believe anything they see on the internet."

"Technological advances mean that it's easier to fool people today than ever before."

1 SPEAKING: talking about popular beliefs

A 2.16 Listen to three conversations about popular beliefs. Make notes. In your own words, explain how the popular beliefs mentioned are false.

1

Great Wall of China

belief: ____________________

reality: ____________________

2

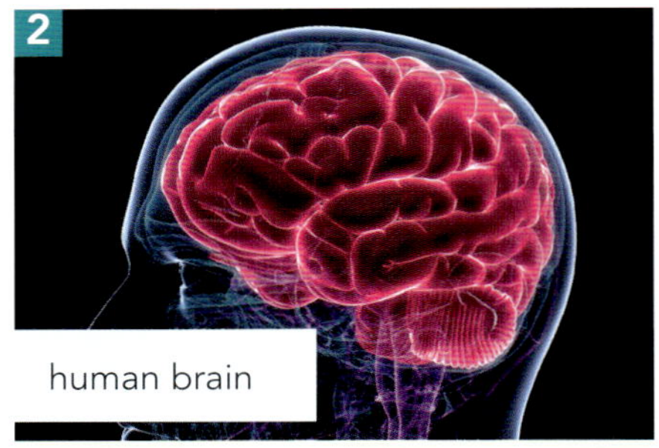

human brain

belief: ____________________

reality: ____________________

B VOCABULARY: FALSEHOOD The words on the left are from the conversations in Exercise A. Choose the word or phrase on the right that has a similar meaning.

1	misconception	false danger / incorrect belief / accepted fact
2	myth	general false belief / accepted fact / proof
3	hoax	trick / research / wrong attitude
4	phony	difficult / very strange / not genuine
5	fake	common / not real / funny
6	gullible	easy to trick / sincere / suspicious

3

shaving

belief: ____________________

reality: ____________________

C VOCABULARY: FALSEHOOD Read the blog entry. Choose the correct options to complete the text.

Home | Blog | About me | Links | Archive

CROP CIRCLES

I can't believe how **(1)** *phony / gullible* some people are! They'll believe anything! Look at crop circles. Strange shapes appear in the crops in a field, and there are two possible explanations. Either they are created by aliens who are trying to communicate with us (although I don't know why they would have the **(2)** *misconception / myth* that we use circles in fields to communicate!), or they are a **(3)** *myth / hoax* created by people in the middle of the night using string and planks of wood. I know which explanation I prefer! Come on, people! Of course they're **(4)** *fake / gullible*! Do you honestly think that aliens would choose that method of communication, rather than, say, just coming down and saying hi? If you believe this **(5)** *misconception / myth*, then you probably also believe that you can save the world or cure disease by sharing a post through social media. Get real and stop listening to this nonsense!

D Choose one statement. Take notes about whether you agree with it or not.

- The 1969 moon landings were fake and never really happened.
- Watching too much TV will permanently damage your eyesight.

E **Independent Speaking** Work in pairs. Talk about whether you believe the statement you chose. Give reasons.

2 GRAMMAR: inversion with negative expressions

A LANGUAGE IN CONTEXT Read the article. Explain what a *conspiracy theory* is in your own words.

CONSPIRACY THEORIES

No sooner does something major happen than people come up with a conspiracy theory explaining who was *really* behind the event and what *really* happened. President Kennedy wasn't assassinated by one man. The moon landings never happened. The simple truth is never enough for the theorists. **Not only** are the rest of us wrong, but we are being fooled by "them," whether it's the government, the secret service, or some other shadowy group. We think we're safe; **little** do we know "they" are spying on all of us. According to the theorists, **only when** we all realize the truth will we be out of danger. It seems that some people have a strong need to disbelieve everything that they are told. **Rarely** do they realize how full of holes their alternative explanations really are.

NOTICE!

Look at the words and phrases in bold. What do you notice about the word order in the rest of the sentence?

B ANALYZE Read the article in Exercise A again.

Form Complete the table with the words in bold from the article.

negative expression + auxiliary verb + subject

phrases referring to time	*other negative expressions*
Hardly had the event happened **when** …	Never have I heard such nonsense.
Barely had the event happened **when** …	Seldom have I heard such nonsense.
Scarcely had the event happened **when** …	**(4)** ______ have I heard such nonsense.
(1) ______ had the event happened **than** …	**(5)** ______ did I realize how wrong I was.
phrases with only	Under no circumstances will I accept that theory.
(2) ______ did we land on the moon, but we also …	
(3) ______ I saw the photos did I realize …	
Only if you have an open mind will you realize the truth.	

Function Choose the correct option to complete each rule.

1 We use inversions after negative adverbials ______.
 a) for emphasis b) as exclamations c) to be polite
2 They are generally quite ______ structures and usually occur in writing.
 a) formal b) informal c) unusual

C PRACTICE Rewrite each sentence as an inversion, starting with the words given.

1 I have rarely heard such a ridiculous theory.
 Seldom ______
2 They will never admit what really happened.
 Under no circumstances ______
3 Immediately after I began to talk, he interrupted me with his own theory.
 No ______
4 Your theory is illogical and it also ignores the evidence.
 Not ______
5 You'll only come to the right conclusion if you examine the evidence.
 Only ______

WATCH OUT!

✘ Under no circumstances you should believe this conspiracy theory!
✓ Under no circumstances should you believe this conspiracy theory!

D NOW YOU DO IT Write a short paragraph giving your opinion of conspiracy theories. Include three sentences with inversions and cover these points:

- whether you think most conspiracy theories are correct
- why conspiracy theories appeal to some people
- any dangers you can see in accepting conspiracy theories

3 READING: a wiki entry

A Read the introductory paragraph. For what reasons might you use snopes.com to verify information?

WikiWorld

Home **Discussion**

[1]Snopes.com [edit paragraph]
Snopes.com, whose tag line is "Rumor Has It," is a website devoted to checking the validity of popular myths, rumors, and legends, including common misconceptions and stories that circulate on the internet or get passed around by email. Snopes was founded in 1995 by Barbara and David Mikkelson, who still run the site today.

B Read the rest of the wiki entry. Decide if the statements below the entry are *T* (true), *F* (false), or *NM* (not mentioned).

[2]History [edit paragraph]
"Snopes" was David's old internet name, and that in turn came from the name of a family that appears in several books by American writer William Faulkner. The Mikkelsons decided to use the name when they launched the site in 1997. The site, located at www.snopes.com, owned and operated entirely by the Mikkelsons, who pay most of their operating costs through online advertising.

[3]How it works [edit paragraph]
People who want to verify or disprove a rumor or story email their query to the Snopes site, and the Mikkelsons research it. They post the story on the site and label it true, false, or undetermined or unverifiable if they can't prove or disprove it. Not only the Mikkelsons debunk or confirm stories, but they also aim to thoroughly research the question and provide evidence and references for their claims. Snopes has become so well-known that people use it as verb: "Before I dismiss that story, I'll Snopes it." In fact, some email hoxes now add a line to their story saying something like "Checked out on Snopes" as fake support.

[4]Reputation [edit paragraph]
In recent years, Snopes has been accused having a politically liberal bias. The organization FactCheck.org in 2009 conducted their own investigation and could not find any confirmation of the charge. "You'd be hard-pressed to find two more apolitical people," says David. Both the Mikkelsons also encourage people to learn how to do their own fact-checking and not to be too gullible when they encounter information.

1 David Mikkelson changed his name in order to set up snopes.com anonymously. *T / F / NM*
2 The Mikkelsons email experts to ask their opinions on stories. *T / F / NM*
3 Some people think Snopes is biased against conservative politicians. *T / F / NM*
4 The Mikkelsons hold strong political views. *T / F / NM*

C Read the wiki entry again. Underline the fact that needs to be checked and corrected. Correct the three grammar mistakes and one spelling mistake in the entry.

D VOCABULARY: WORD FORMS (PROVING AND DISPROVING) Complete the table. Then find words from the wiki entry on page 120 to check your answers.

	noun	verb	adjective	participial adjective
proving a claim	validation/ (1) ______	validate	valid	validated, validating
	verification	(2) ______	verifiable	verified
	(3) ______	(4) ______	–	confirmed
	(5) ______	support	supportable	supported, supporting
	proof	(6) ______	provable	proved/proven
disproving a claim	dismissal	(7) ______	dismissive	dismissed
	–	(8) ______	–	debunked, debunking
	disproval	(9) ______	–	disproved/disproven

E VOCABULARY: WORD FORMS (PROVING AND DISPROVING) Choose the correct word form to complete each sentence.

1 It's important to find independent *valid* / *validation* of facts asserted in an article.
2 It isn't necessary for friends to *confirm* / *confirmed* every story they tell you.
3 When you make a claim, you should always *support* / *supported* it with examples.
4 Some information just isn't *verify* / *verifiable*. There's really no way to know if it's true or not.
5 If lots of people you know have *dismiss* / *dismissed* a claim, it probably isn't true.
6 If a claim is supported with scientific *proof* / *provable*, you can assume it's true.

F Work in pairs. Discuss whether you agree or disagree with the sentences in Exercise E.

4 WRITING: a wiki entry

A wiki is a website where users create and edit articles collaboratively. One person posts an article, and then other people add more information and correct mistakes if necessary. When collaborating on a wiki, do not use a biased point of view, or your contribution may be deleted. Also, cite your sources wherever possible, so that people can check what you've written.

A Write a 1–2 paragraph entry for DebunkerWiki, a website which explores the truth behind popular beliefs. Write about one of these popular beliefs or another popular belief. Explain whether the belief is true or false.

- Drinking coffee helps you to study.
- Playing violent video games causes people to act violently.
- Goldfish have a short memory of only a few seconds.

B Work in groups. Pass your entries around. Each group member reads each entry and suggests changes, such as making the entry more objective, offering more support, or correcting language.

C Read your article after everyone in your group has read and changed it. Discuss whether you think the changes have improved the article or whether you prefer the original version.

5 GRAMMAR: ellipsis and substitution

A 2.17 **LANGUAGE IN CONTEXT** Listen to the conversation. Explain what *phishing* is in your own words.

Keaton: Hey, Joel. Haven't seen you around. How are things?
Joel: Oh, hi, Keaton. Not so good, actually.
Keaton: Why's that?
Joel: I was the victim of an internet scam. Cost me a lot of money. I got a phishing email and I clicked on it. Heard of those?
Keaton: Phishing? Yes, I believe so. It's like identity theft, isn't it?
Joel: Yeah, I guess so. Someone sends an email that looks as if it comes from a bank. The person receiving the email thinks it's genuine. It tells you to click on a link and when you do so, it takes you to a website that looks like a bank's website. It tells you to enter your password and, in doing so, you're giving it away to whoever runs the site.
Keaton: And then the password entered is used to access your account and take your money. You going to get any of it back?
Joel: I hope so!

NOTICE!

Find and underline at least two examples of statements that seem to be incomplete sentences because initial words are missing. Is the meaning of the sentence different without the initial words?

B ANALYZE Read the conversation in Exercise A again.

Form Complete the table with examples from the conversation.

Ellipsis: *missing initial unstressed words*	**Ellipsis:** *reduced relative structures*
Haven't seen you around. Not so good, actually. **(1)** ___________ **(2)** ___________	**(3)** ___________ thinks it's genuine … **(4)** ___________ is used to access your account …

Substitution: *expressions using* **so**
… when you **(5)** ___________, it takes you …
It tells you to enter your password and **(6)** ___________, …

Positive	**Negative**
Yeah, I **(7)** ___________. I hope so!	I don't think so. I hope not!

WATCH OUT!

✗ Ever you fallen for any scams in the past?
✓ Ever fallen for any scams in the past?

Function Choose the correct options to complete the explanation.
In ellipsis, we **(1)** *leave out* / *add* some words where these are obvious from context.
In substitution, we use words such as **(2)** *because* / *so* in place of other words and phrases. We use it to avoid repeating ourselves.

C PRACTICE Find and correct six mistakes with ellipsis and substitution in the text.

Had you any suspicious emails recently? Perhaps the sender claims to be a relative of a famous person and they will pay you to help transfer money. And the amount of money that promised is in the millions. This email scam has been around for years. The person who sending the email probably claims they need to send money outside their country but can't do because of political problems there. The email asks you to help and says that doing so you will earn a reward. But first, you just have to pay a small administration fee and send your details. Of course, once you've done it so, you never see the fee again and are at risk of identity theft. The best way to deal with these emails is to delete them immediately and forget about them.

D NOW YOU DO IT You manage social media for a website that promotes online safety. Write a short post about each topic (max. 140 characters).

- identify theft
- online scams
- phishing

6 PRONUNCIATION: thought groups

A 2.18 **Listen to the sentences. Notice how the speaker pauses between the thought groups, and that commas are often used to mark thought groups.**

1 According to a survey by Gartner, / a leading information technology research and advisory company, / 4.3% of targets of email hoaxes / lost money.
2 Regular mass email marketing campaigns, / on the other hand, / have a success rate / of only 1.5%.

B 2.19 **Work in pairs. Listen and practice the sentences. Pay attention to the thought groups.**

1 To protect yourself from hoaxes, / don't ever click on links / in emails from an unknown sender.
2 In addition, / don't give out passwords / or other personal information / over the phone.
3 If you think a company is really trying to contact you / —your bank, / for example— / hang up / and call them back yourself.

7 LISTENING: difficult situations

When you are talking with two or more native speakers, they may speak quickly or use vocabulary, slang, or even grammar that you don't know. When you can't understand something important, stop the conversation and ask for help.

A **Work in groups. Discuss the questions.**

- Which social networking sites (e.g., Facebook, Twitter) do you use, if any?
- Did you join any of them because your friends were already using them and asked you to join?
- Have you ever bought something, or downloaded an app or music track, because someone recommended it via social media? If so, why did the recommendation make you want to get it?

B 2.20 **Listen to a discussion. What, if anything, caused listening problems for you? Check the appropriate column.**

	Speed	One word or phrase	One or more sentences
Part 1			
Part 2			
Part 3			
Part 4			
Part 5			

C **Listen again. Check the sentence you heard.**

Part 1:
☐ a) Sorry, a what?
☐ b) Sorry, what for?

Part 2:
☐ a) I don't know what "viral marketing" means.
☐ b) I don't know how you mean "viral marketing."

Part 3:
☐ a) Can you say that again more slowly?
☐ b) Sorry, can you say that again?

Part 4:
☐ a) I'm sorry, I'm lost.
☐ b) OK, you just lost me.

Part 5:
☐ a) What does that mean?
☐ b) What is the meaning?

D **Work in pairs. Discuss the questions with your partner.**

1 Do you find it easy to stop conversations and ask for help? Why or why not?
2 Are there times when it's better not to stop a conversation? If so, when?
3 What do you find most difficult about listening to native speakers?

lifeSkills

EVALUATING INTERNET SOURCE RELIABILITY

- Know what questions to ask in order to determine a website's reliability.
- Find the answers to the questions.
- Use the answers to determine whether the website is reliable.

A Check the questions you usually ask when you do research online.

1 ☐ What type of website is it (e.g., academic, a personal blog, a political organization)?
2 ☐ Who is the author of the specific information you want to use?
3 ☐ Is there a clear point of view or bias? If so, what is it?
4 ☐ If there is a claim, is there evidence to support it?
5 ☐ Are there references or links to other sources?
6 ☐ Can the information be verified? If so, how?
7 ☐ How current is the information?

B Work in groups. Discuss why each of the questions in Exercise A is important.

C Match the numbers of the questions from Exercise A with the ways to find the answers.

a) Look for emotionally charged language. Check if the website lists goals or a mission. ☐
b) Look for links (often underlined or in another color) to other sites. Check for sections at the end of an article called References, Bibliography, or For Further Reading. ☐
c) Check under the title of the article for a name. Does the name link to any further information about the author, or is there an author bio (biography) on the page? ☐
d) Check if enough specific information is given (e.g., places, names, dates) that you could put into a search engine to verify the information somewhere else. ☐
e) Look for a date at the top or bottom of the home page. Look for a date near the author's name or the title of an individual article. ☐
f) Look for the internet domain (.edu = an academic institution; .org = an organization; .gov = an official government site). Read the Home or About Us page. ☐
g) Check if the main points are supported by statistics, quotes from experts, examples, or logical reasoning. ☐

D Work in pairs. Read the article on page 125 and answer the questions from Exercise A. If you can't answer a question, discuss how you could find the answer.

OBESITY PANACEA

HOME | NEWS | LIFESTYLE & HEALTH | MESSAGE BOARD

DO DIET SOFT DRINKS LEAD TO OBESITY?

[1]Are diet soft drinks bad for you? I received this question from Perry Romanowski after it came up on his blog and I thought it would make an excellent topic for today. More specifically, I would like to discuss the relationship between diet soft drinks and obesity.

[2]At first, I did not expect there to be any relationship between diet soft drinks and obesity—if they contain no calories, they can't possibly contribute to a positive energy balance, right? Early studies of calorie-free sweeteners like aspartame seem to support that position. For example, a review article from 1991 suggests that "aspartame-sweetened foods or drinks is [sic] associated with either no change or a reduction in food intake." However, more recent studies suggest that the issue is not quite so simple.

[3]An article published in 2008 by Sharon Fowler in the journal *Obesity* suggests that individuals who consume diet soft drinks are at dramatically increased risk of being overweight or obese than those who do not consume diet soft drinks. For example, over an eight-year period, individuals who consumed just three diet soft drinks a week were 40% more likely to be overweight or obese than those who consumed none. The risk continued to increase dramatically with increased diet soft drink intake, and was independent of other factors like exercise, smoking, and socioeconomic status.

[4]The Fowler study doesn't prove that diet soft drinks cause obesity (people who drink more diet soft drinks may also have other behaviors that put them at increased risk for weight gain), but they are still pretty surprising. While diet soft drinks may themselves be free of calories, recent evidence suggests that they may increase calorie intake at future meals. For example, when rats are given access to unlimited amounts of food, those who are used to consuming calorie-free drinks eat dramatically more than those who are used to consuming drinks flavored with sugar. It may be that calorie-free drinks impair the body's ability to anticipate the calorie content of a given meal, eventually resulting in increased calorie intake and weight gain. Others have suggested that calorie-free sweeteners like aspartame may also increase appetite at future meals.

[5]So, while it is not yet completely clear if diet soft drinks *cause* obesity, there are some good reasons to limit their intake.

www.obesitypanacea.com

HOW TO SAY IT

The main point made by the author is that …

I think more evidence supporting the claim is needed and …

I think this source should/shouldn't/can/can't be believed because …

This article could/can't be considered very reliable/biased because …

E Work with another pair. Discuss how reliable you think the information in the article is. Explain why.

F Discuss the questions.

1 What have you learned about online sources and their reliability?
2 Do you think you will be able to judge online sources better in the future?

REFLECT … How can the skill of evaluating internet source reliability be useful to you in **Work & Career** & **Self & Society**?

RESEARCH …

Choose a topic that interests you. Find at least three different websites on the topic. Evaluate their reliability using the criteria in Exercise A and decide which one you consider to be the most reliable source on that topic, and which is the most unreliable. In your next lesson, explain to the class the reasons for your evaluation of them.

Language wrap-up

1 VOCABULARY

A Complete the sentences with the words from the box. (6 points)

fake   gullible   hoax   misconception   myth   phony

1 That story about the fried mouse is just an urban ________.
2 The idea that you can't go swimming for 30 minutes after you eat is a common ________.
3 The picture of the UFO was completely ________. It was just a model airplane.
4 Some people claim that only ________ people are fooled by internet phishing scams.
5 The email that said I'd won the lottery was a ________. I hadn't even entered a lottery.
6 It turned out that the email was ________. There isn't a company with that name.

B Complete the words. (4 points)

1 The researchers finally debunk____ the rumor.
2 Have you verif____ that claim?
3 I will believe you if you can offer me some kind of valid____.
4 After receiving confirm____, the newspaper decided to run the story on the front page.

8–10 correct: I can talk about falsehood, and use the correct word endings to talk about proving and disproving information.
0–7 correct: Look again at Sections 1 and 3 on pages 118, 120, and 121.   SCORE: /10

2 GRAMMAR

A Rewrite the sentences. Start with the words and phrases given. (6 points)

1 As soon as I got home, I saw the email. (*no sooner*)
____
2 I read about Kennedy's assassination and I saw a documentary about it. (*not only*)
____
3 I have never heard such a ridiculous explanation before. (*never*)
____
4 I didn't realize it was, in fact, a phishing email. (*little*)
____
5 Immediately after I clicked on the link, my computer froze. (*scarcely*)
____
6 They will only access your account if you give them your password. (*only*)
____

B Rewrite the sentences using ellipsis and substitution where possible. (4 points)

1 Have you ever received a phishing email? Do you know someone who has gotten one?
____
2 I should get all my money back, or at least I hope I get all my money back.
____
3 The person who is making the claim has not presented a case that is supported by facts.
____
4 Anyone who uses the lab must have a pass that is signed by the director.
____

8–10 correct: I can use inversions with negative expressions and ellipsis and substitution.
0–7 correct: Look again at Sections 2 and 5 on pages 119 and 122.   SCORE: /10

SPEAKING WORKSHOP

Responding with an opinion

A 2.21 **Listen to someone answering the question. Make a note of the speaker's main points. In pairs, compare your notes.**

Some people believe that all students should be taught about online scams and dangers at school. Others argue that schools should only be responsible for teaching academic topics. Which view do you agree with most? Include details and examples in your explanation.

B Listen again for phrases the speaker uses to express her opinion. Write a word or short phrase in each blank.

1 In general, I am ________________ the opinion that …
2 Not only ________________ that, but I would also argue that …
3 The ________________ reason for my opinion is …
4 My opinion is also ________________ my own experience of …
5 I have no ________________ that …
6 However, it ________________ to me that …

C Answer the questions.

1 Why might some people believe that websites like Wikipedia are unreliable?
____
2 Why might some people believe that websites like Wikipedia are reliable?
____
3 Which view do you most agree with?
____
4 What is the primary reason for your opinion?
____
5 What are the secondary reasons for your opinion?
____
6 Describe any relevant personal experience you have to support your opinion.
____

D In small groups, present your opinion about the question in the box.

Some people believe that collaboratively edited online information sources such as Wikipedia are as reliable as traditional encyclopedias. Others argue that the information found on such websites is unreliable. Which view do you agree with most? Include details and examples in your explanation.

HOW ARE YOU DOING?

- ◯ I have made clear which view I agree with.
- ◯ I have outlined the primary reason and any secondary reasons for my opinion.
- ◯ I have used any relevant personal experience I have to support my opinion.

UNIT 11 MUSIC TO MY EARS

IN THIS UNIT YOU

- learn language to talk about music, musicians, and the music industry
- read an article about a famous musician who did something unusual
- make polite refusals
- listen to a discussion about musical intelligence
- write an opinion about music sharing
- learn to identify bias in things people say and write
- watch a video about a street busker

READING
understanding intent

Do writers in your language use italics, quotation marks, and bold type? If so, what do they use them for?

SPEAKING
softening language for refusals

What do you think "softening language" is? Give some examples.

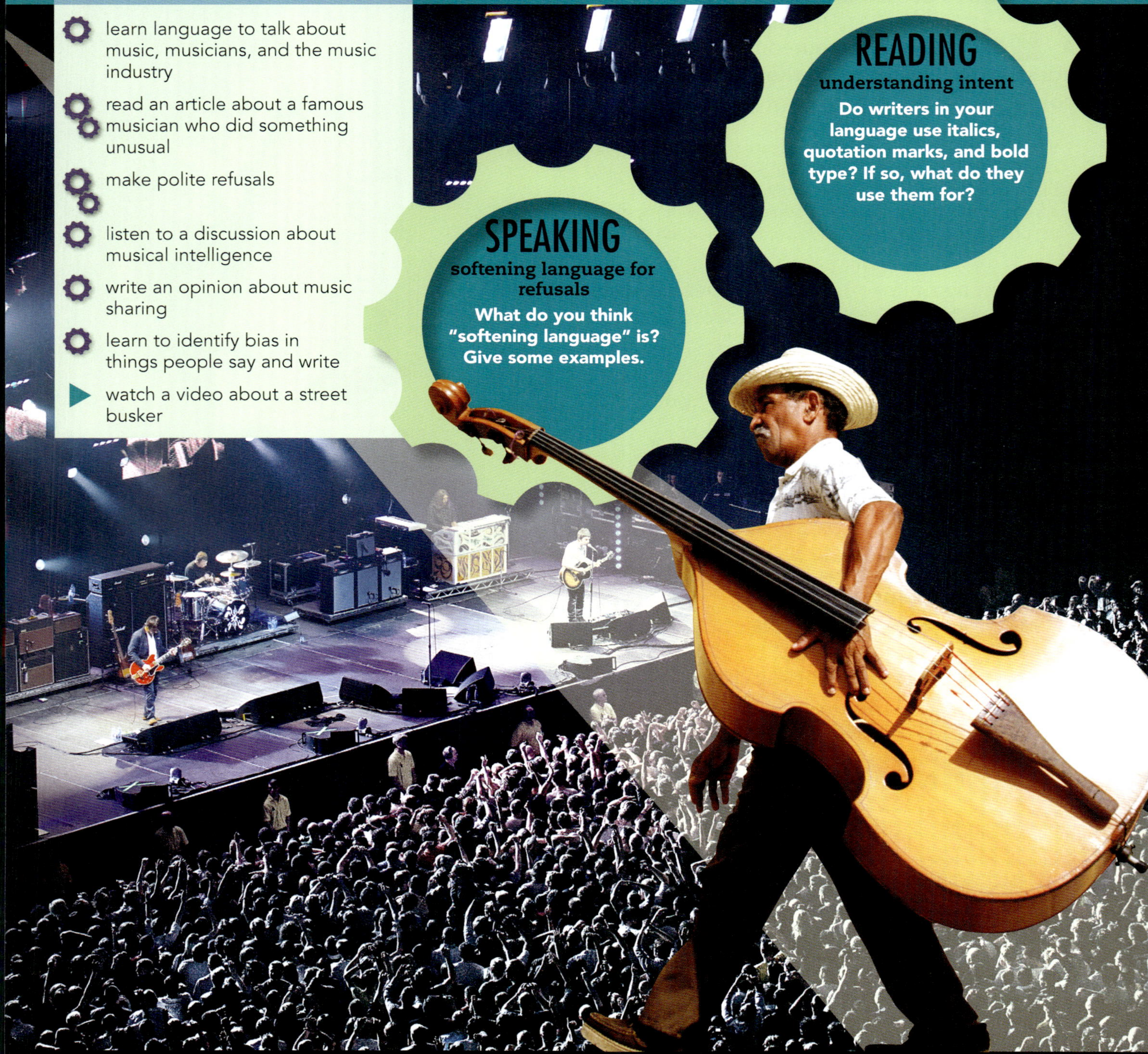

LIFE SKILLS

SELF & SOCIETY

identifying bias Who might have the strongest opinions about free music downloads?

- music companies
- musicians
- the general public
- music-sharing website owners

A Work in groups. Read the quotes about music. Discuss what each one means and whether or not you agree with it.

"It's no good pretending that any relationship has a future if your record collections disagree violently or if your favorite films wouldn't even speak to each other if they met at a party."
Nick Hornby, *High Fidelity*

"We should consider every day lost on which we have not danced at least once."
Friedrich Nietzsche

"Where words leave off, music begins."
Heinrich Heine

"The only truth is music."
Jack Kerouac

"There's only one type of music and that's good music, no matter what genre it is."
will.i.am

B With your group, create a quote about music. Read it to your class. Take a class vote on the most memorable quotes from the class.

1 READING: understanding intent page 106

Writers have an overall intent when they write a text, but they also have specific aims (e.g., to argue or entertain). They express these aims through techniques. For example, they may use italics or quotation marks to emphasize certain words. They may also use direct speech to personalize the writing or to create a sense of drama.

A Read the article. Then discuss the questions as a class.

1 Would you have stopped to listen? Why or why not?
2 What do you think the writer's overall intent is?

DOES BEAUTY TRANSCEND?

[1]Street musicians, or **(1)** "buskers," play for free, hoping to earn a few dollars for a meal, or in a wildly improbable scenario, to be noticed and liked by someone in the music industry. Few people stop to listen.

[2]One day in Washington, D.C., I was hurrying to catch the subway. I was with a colleague, and as we walked along the underground passage of the subway, we could hear a lively violin piece coming from somewhere beyond us. We rounded a corner and saw a young man in jeans with an open violin case at his feet. There was one dollar in the case. "Whooo-wee," said Joe eloquently. **(2)** "That boy **(3)** *really* has what it takes to play the fiddle."

[3]Joe is from Louisiana, which explains why he would refer to what I later learned was a $3.5 million violin as a **(4)** "fiddle." It turned out that the "fiddle player" in the subway had been none other than premier violinist Joshua Bell, who had, in fact, recently played in the Boston Symphony Hall, and people had paid over $100 a seat for the privilege of hearing him. Bell was posing as a busker that day in the subway for an experiment set up by a Washington newspaper to find out whether people recognize and appreciate talent and beauty taken out of context.

[4]So, as our title asks, does beauty transcend? If it is moved from an elegant context to a mundane one, will people still recognize it as something extraordinary? Apparently not. In the 45 minutes that Joshua Bell performed difficult and intricate classical pieces, 27 people gave him money, for a grand total of $32.17. Only seven actually took the performance seriously enough to stop to listen.

[5]After reading the newspaper article, I told a friend who works in marketing about the experiment. He said that you have to take into account the fact that people are often too busy to do a lot of analysis. They want things explained and categorized for them. He cited market surveys in which people classify one of two identical products as being better than the other when it is in a nicer, classier package.

[6]The fact is that we take it for granted that **(5)** "what you see is what you get," so if a musician looks like a busker and is playing where one would expect a busker to play, then logic dictates that he is a struggling street musician and not a world-class violinist. We toss him a few coins, certain that we have done our good deed for the day, never imagining that we may have missed a once-in-a lifetime performance simply through not bothering to think out of the box!

B Why did the writer use quotation marks or italics for the numbered words and phrases? Match each word or phrase (1–5) with one of the purposes (a–e).

a) To emphasize a word or phrase ☐
b) To introduce a new word or phrase ☐
c) To indicate irony or sarcasm ☐
d) To quote someone directly ☐
e) To quote a well-known phrase ☐

C **VOCABULARY: IDIOMATIC EXPRESSIONS WITH *TAKE*** Complete the sentences with appropriate forms of the underlined expressions from the article in Exercise A.

1 The quote was ________________ by the press, which changed its meaning.
2 Most professional musicians ________________ their music very ________________.
3 Only a few musicians ________________ to become stars.
4 Pop stars who have long careers never ________________ their fame ________________.
5 We think musicians have a great life, but we don't ________________ the difficulty of constant travel.

D **VOCABULARY: IDIOMATIC EXPRESSIONS WITH *TAKE*** Work in groups. Discuss the questions.

1 Do you take street musicians seriously, or do you assume that they're not good enough to be professionals?
2 What factors should people who are thinking of becoming professional musicians take into account?

2 GRAMMAR: past tense for unreal situations

A **LANGUAGE IN CONTEXT** Read the extract from an article. Why do you think the musicians decided to perform on the street?

In this month's issue ...

Suppose you were walking down the street and you heard a street performer playing. Would you take him or her seriously and stop to listen? Unless you really liked the song, you probably wouldn't stop. Well, maybe it's time you stopped taking street performers for granted. A number of famous performers started their careers on street corners, including Bob Dylan, Joni Mitchell, and Tracy Chapman. Even after becoming famous, some musicians have performed on the streets, including Sting and Paul McCartney. Just think—next time you want to see a show and wish you had tickets, take time out to listen to the street performer outside the venue. Imagine how you would feel if you stopped to listen and saw that it was your favorite musician. What if that happened? Wouldn't that be amazing?

NOTICE!

Which events in the text are hypothetical or not real? Underline the verbs that are used to talk about these events.

B **ANALYZE** Read the extract in Exercise A again.

Form & Function Complete the table with examples from the text.

verb or phrase + subject + past tense verb *Suppose ...* *it's time ...* *What if ...*	**(1)** Suppose _______________ down the street. **(2)** ... maybe it's time _______________ taking ... **(3)** What if that _______________?
subject + *wish* + subject + past tense verb	You wish you had tickets.
***if/unless* + past tense verb + *would/wouldn't* + verb**	**(4)** Imagine how you would feel if _______________ to listen... **(5)** Unless _______________ the song, you probably _______________.

C **PRACTICE** Rewrite the sentences using the words and phrases in parentheses.

1 I would only give a street performer money if I really liked the song. (*unless*)
____
2 Imagine that you wanted to become a musician. (*suppose*)
____
3 I really think we should ban street performers. (*it's time*)
____
4 I wouldn't give a street performer money unless they had talent. (*if*)
____
5 Imagine that you met your favorite performer at a party. (*What if*)
____

WATCH OUT!

✗ I wish people give more money to street performers.
✓ I wish people _______ more money to street performers.

D **NOW YOU DO IT** Work in pairs. Use the phrases to write statements about music/musicians. Then discuss with your partner.

Suppose / What if ...   *How would you feel if... ?*   *I wish ...*   *It's time ...*

3 LISTENING: to an informal discussion

A 2.22 Read the statements and decide whether you think each one is *T* (true) or *F* (false). Then listen to the first part of a discussion and check your answers.

Musical intelligence …

1. is one of a number of different intelligences. *T / F*
2. is the same thing as musical talent. *T / F*
3. can be useful outside the area of music. *T / F*
4. can be developed through training. *T / F*

B 2.23 Listen to the rest of the discussion. As you listen, take notes in your notebook on the main points each speaker makes about himself/herself. Then compare notes with a partner.

C Take the quiz. Rate yourself on each aspect of musical intelligence from 1 (=not true for you) to 10 (=true for you). Then add the numbers for your total score.

☐ I am very aware of sounds in the environment around me.	☐ I am a good singer or play a musical instrument well.
☐ I easily remember song melodies.	☐ I can identify when an instrument or a singer is off-key.
☐ I work well with music playing in the background.	☐ I like many different types of music.
☐ I often sing, whistle, or tap a song with my fingers/a pen/etc.	☐ I am a good listener in general.

TOTAL
low musical intelligence: < 32
average musical intelligence: 32–56
high musical intelligence: > 56

Back Reset Submit

D Work in pairs. Compare your answers and total scores. Discuss the role you think musical intelligence plays in your life.

4 GRAMMAR: cleft sentences

A LANGUAGE IN CONTEXT Read about the group of musicians. What reasons for their success does the writer present?

NOTICE!

Look at the underlined sentence. Can you change the word order to form a new sentence with the same meaning?

SPOTLight

Joe Jackson's Vision by Amir Faizal

The Jackson Five were one of the biggest pop groups of the 1970s. It was this group that launched the career of Michael Jackson. One reason why they were so successful was that they appealed to people of different generations all over the world. This success was not purely the result of musical talent, however. The Jackson Five story shows that what is really needed to develop musical ability is long hours of rehearsal. <u>The person who pushed them to succeed was their strict father, Joseph Jackson</u>. It was he who made the boys practice every evening after school. Joe Jackson's relationship with his sons might have suffered, but what really made the group a success was his vision.

B ANALYZE Read the text in Exercise A again.

Function

To emphasize specific information, we can change the usual structure of a sentence and use two clauses instead of one. This is called a cleft (divided) sentence.

Form Complete the table with examples from the text.

Non-cleft form	Cleft form
This group launched the career of Michael Jackson.	*It* + *be* + noun + relative clause: (1) ______
They were so successful because they appealed to people … Their strict father, Joseph Jackson, pushed them to succeed.	subject + relative clause + *be* + complement (2) ______ (3) ______
His vision was what made the group a success.	*What* + verb phrase + clause (4) ______

The first two forms of cleft sentences can be used interchangeably:
It was Mike who told me about this album.
The person who told me about this album was Mike.
You can delete the relative pronoun when it comes before a subject, but not when it comes before a verb.

C PRACTICE Rewrite each sentence as a cleft sentence, using the words in parentheses. If the relative pronoun can be omitted, put it in parentheses.

1 I admire Justin Timberlake because he is always reinventing himself as an artist. (*who*)
One person (who) I admire is Justin Timberlake because he is always reinventing himself as an artist.

2 Jay Z is so successful because he understands the music industry. (*why*)
The reason ______.

3 Elvis Presley lived in a place called Graceland. (*where*)
The place ______.

4 The concert took place on my birthday. (*when*)
The day ______.

5 I like music these days because of the wide variety of styles. (*is*)
______

6 I like the lyrics on this album. (*What*)
______

WATCH OUT!

✗ The person who started the band was Bob Martin. ➜ The person started the band was Bob Martin.

✓ The day when I saw the concert was a Friday. ➜ The day I saw the concert was a Friday.

D NOW YOU DO IT Work in pairs. Talk about musicians you admire.

The person who I admire most in the music world is …
The reason why he/she impresses me is …
It was when I heard …
The thing that I like about him/her is …
What I like about him/her is …

5 SPEAKING: softening language for refusals

We sometimes want to refuse a request because we would rather not do it for ethical, professional, or personal reasons. We often do several different things to "soften" our refusal so that it doesn't sound impolite. First, we use phrases that do not include the word "no." Second, we give reasons for our refusal. Third, we try to suggest alternatives that might be acceptable to the other person.

A Look at the list of things friends might ask or suggest that you do. Check the ones you would be happy to do.

- ☐ copy music from your computer to theirs
- ☐ download pirated music
- ☐ make a copy of your concert ticket so they could go to the concert for free
- ☐ make a recording of a concert so that you and your friends can listen to it
- ☐ make a recording of a concert to sell online

B 2.24 Listen to the conversation. Underline the item in Exercise A that Nicole wants Bill to do. How does he respond to her request?

C Listen again. Then complete the phrases that Bill uses. Do you think most young people agree with Bill? Why or why not?

Phrases for saying "*no*" or "*probably not*"	Phrases for softening explanations or excuses
I don't know.	The problem/thing is that …
I'm (1) ________.	I feel/think it's just/kind of …
(2) ________, but	To (4) ________, …
(3) ________.	It's (5) ________ …
	It's just my opinion, but …

D Work in pairs. Take turns making requests and refusing politely. Use phrases from Exercise C.

A: *I missed the exam on Friday, and I have to take it on Monday instead. Can you tell me what some of the questions are?*

B: *Uh …, sorry, but I don't really remember any of the questions. It was pretty easy though.*

E VOCABULARY: SHARING MUSIC Match the words and phrases (1–6) with the definitions (a–f).

1	track (*n.*)	a)	the legal right of ownership of a song or movie.
2	copyright (*n.*)	b)	listen to or watch something directly on the internet
3	stream (*v.*)	c)	the crime of making and selling illegal copies of songs, etc.
4	subscribe (*v.*)	d)	a song recorded on a CD or available as a file
5	file sharing (*n.*)	e)	pay a regular fee to receive a service
6	piracy (*n.*)	f)	the process of transferring data from one computer to another via the internet

F VOCABULARY: SHARING MUSIC Work in pairs. Choose a situation from Exercise A. Student A, try to convince Student B to do it. Student B, refuse politely. When you finish, choose another situation and swap roles.

6 PRONUNCIATION: intonation in cleft sentences

A 2.25 **Listen and notice the small pause between the two clauses in each sentence. Then practice saying the sentences.**

1 What I don't like about that group ○ is their violent lyrics.
2 The person who gave me that album ○ was a musician.
3 The reason why I called you ○ was to invite you to a concert.

B 2.26 **Listen to the sentences. Check the sentences that start with rising intonation. Then practice saying the sentences with a partner.**

1 ☐ The singer who I admire the most is Adele.
2 ☐ The place where I saw them in concert was a big stadium.
3 ☐ The year when he won a Grammy was 2014.
4 ☐ What I don't know is when they first sang that song.

7 WRITING: posting an opinion

A Read the post. What points do the writers make for and against file sharing?

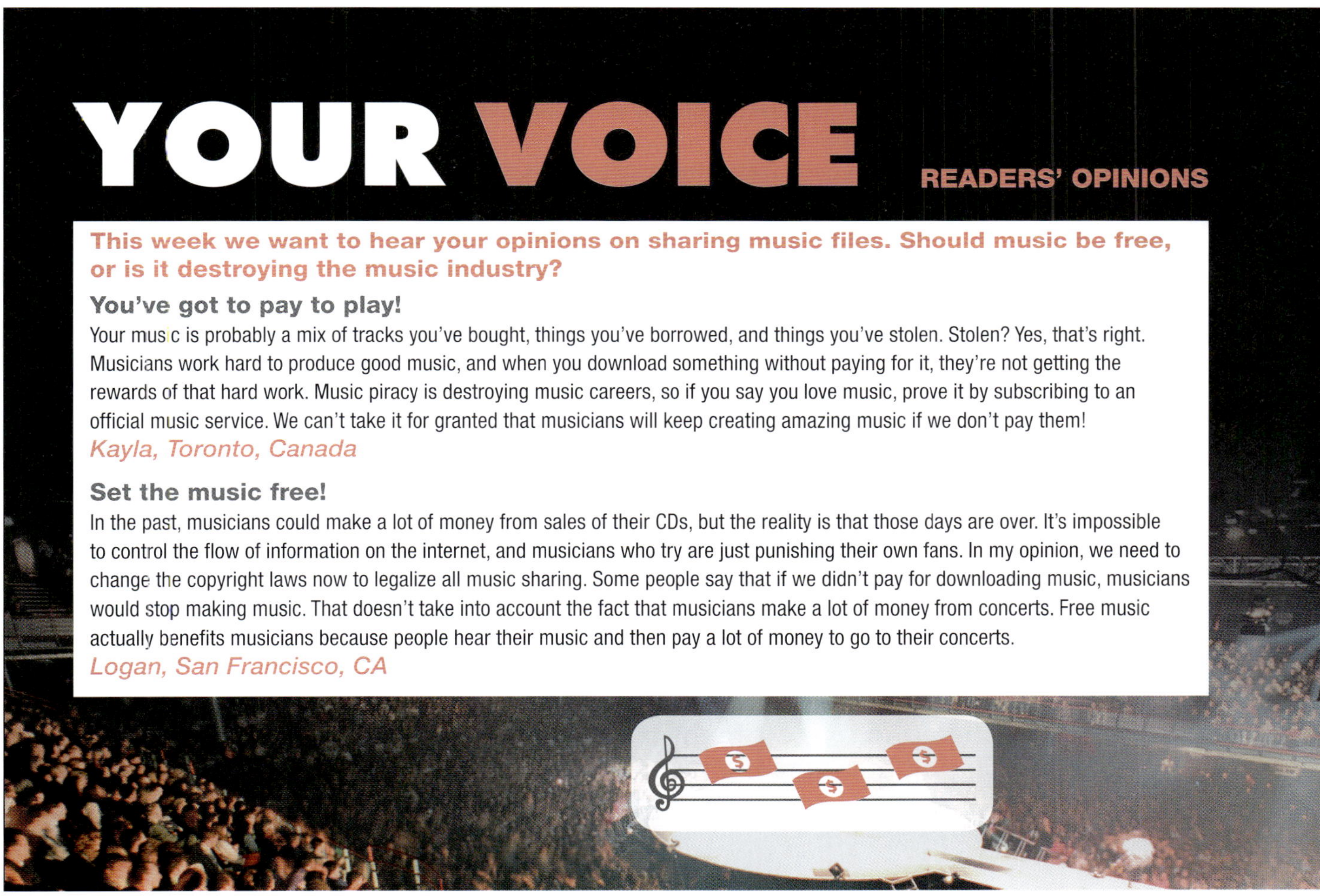

YOUR VOICE

READERS' OPINIONS

This week we want to hear your opinions on sharing music files. Should music be free, or is it destroying the music industry?

You've got to pay to play!

Your music is probably a mix of tracks you've bought, things you've borrowed, and things you've stolen. Stolen? Yes, that's right. Musicians work hard to produce good music, and when you download something without paying for it, they're not getting the rewards of that hard work. Music piracy is destroying music careers, so if you say you love music, prove it by subscribing to an official music service. We can't take it for granted that musicians will keep creating amazing music if we don't pay them!

Kayla, Toronto, Canada

Set the music free!

In the past, musicians could make a lot of money from sales of their CDs, but the reality is that those days are over. It's impossible to control the flow of information on the internet, and musicians who try are just punishing their own fans. In my opinion, we need to change the copyright laws now to legalize all music sharing. Some people say that if we didn't pay for downloading music, musicians would stop making music. That doesn't take into account the fact that musicians make a lot of money from concerts. Free music actually benefits musicians because people hear their music and then pay a lot of money to go to their concerts.

Logan, San Francisco, CA

B Write a response to the two posts above. First, make notes to answer the questions.

1 Which of the two writers do you agree with more?
2 What are the main reasons why you disagree with one of the writers?
3 What are the main reasons why you agree with the other writer?

C Write your response. Use your answers to the questions from Exercise B to guide you.

lifeSkills

IDENTIFYING BIAS

- Understand different types of bias.
- Consider who a writer is and who or what they represent.
- Look at the language a writer uses and what they emphasize or omit in order to decide whether their writing is biased or not.

A Work in pairs. Read the wiki entry about types of bias. Discuss what each type of bias involves. Have you ever heard or seen examples of each type of bias?

bias /ˈbaɪəs/ [SINGULAR/NONCOUNT NOUN] a special interest or tendency to favor a particular person, thing, or opinion
*That judge holds a lot of **bias** toward female vocalists.*

Types of bias

Sometimes writers appear to describe a situation objectively—that is to say, factually—but careful reading can reveal bias. There are a number of different types of bias, some of which are easier to identify than others. When someone is biased against a particular person or social group, they might directly state opinions that make the biased position obvious. However, there are other types of bias that may not be so obvious:

- **Bias by selection of facts**

When writers argue a point of view, they often refer to statistics or to things experts have said. However, bias can often be seen in the statistics or quotations chosen by a writer. A writer may select statistics or information that only support his/her view and omit statistics that do not directly support that point of view.

- **Bias by labeling**

It's possible to detect bias in the terms a writer uses. For example, the same activity could be called "file sharing" or "music piracy," depending on whether you are biased in favor of it or against it.

- **Bias by exaggeration, emphasis, or repetition**

Writers might show their bias by using exaggeration. They might exaggerate the position they support to make it seem better than it is, or the position they are against to make it seem worse than it is. The use of strong language, emphasis, and repetition often demonstrates this kind of bias.

B Each person has an interest in the issue of digital music distribution. In pairs, make notes on how you might expect them to be biased.

Jake: a successful musician

He has made money from selling music, so he might be biased toward protecting his income. He would probably argue that people should continue to pay for downloads. He might ignore the opinions of ordinary music fans and emphasize how difficult it is for musicians to make a living.

Blue: a struggling musician who is trying to break into the music business

Megan: an executive who works for a large record label

Luise: a music fan

Self and Society
Work and Career
Study and Learning

C Read the extracts. Match them with the people from Exercise B who probably wrote them. Discuss the answers and reasons as a class.

1 ______________

It's time the music industry learned that they're never going to be able to control the distribution of music. I've read that 67% of downloaders don't care about copyright, and it's going to be impossible to change the minds of that many people. Some people argue that music streaming services are very cheap. Still, they cost around $20 a month and not everyone in the world has an extra $20 lying around, especially young people! Music wants to be free. Musicians are just going to have to learn to make their living from performing.

2 ______________

It takes extremely long hours on the road and years of commitment to make it in music. People have no idea how hard musicians work! The reason why so much music exists is that musicians get paid for creating it. If artists are forced to give up their careers because they can't make enough money, we will all suffer. The bottom line is that music has to be paid for and not stolen. We can't just have anarchy in the digital world! We're in danger of letting piracy destroy the music industry in this country.

3 ______________

One of the more interesting developments of the last few years is the rise of streaming services such as Spotify. These services offer thousands of tracks—all the music anyone could possibly want. When you subscribe, you can stream tracks to your computer or smartphone, and subscriptions cost on average only about $15–$20 per month. It has the potential to get people off the habit of stealing music, while at the same time providing important income to artists, many of whom aren't particularly rich. We're always going to need ways of supporting young talent.

4 ______________

Many people ask me what I think about people sharing music online, and I've thought about it a lot. On the one hand, I can see that technology is powerful and useful, but at the same time I understand that artists and labels need income. I guess the days of making a fortune off your CDs are gone, but people are probably prepared to pay something for music. In fact, there are now so many sites that offer inexpensive legal downloads that I don't think there's a real reason for downloading illegally anymore.

HOW TO SAY IT

The thing that I notice about this text is that …

The reason why I say this one is very / pretty / not very biased is …

D Work in pairs. Read the extracts again. Discuss whether each one is very biased, slightly biased, or not particularly biased.

E Look back at the types of bias mentioned in Exercise A. As a class, discuss whether the extracts include any of these types of bias.

F Discuss the questions.

1 Is it easy to identify bias? How and in what situations will you try to identify it in the future?
2 Is bias always a bad thing? If not, in what situations might it be acceptable?

REFLECT … How can the skill of identifying bias be useful to you in **Study & Learning** and **Work & Career**?

RESEARCH …

Find an article on a topic that involves different points of view. The topic can be related to music or it can be a different topic. Read the article carefully and underline any examples of bias. Tell your class what the article is about and why you think it is biased or not.

Language wrap-up

1 VOCABULARY

Complete the paragraph with the words and phrases from the box. You will need to change the form of some of the words and phrases. (10 points)

copyright   file sharing   have what it takes   piracy   stream   subscribe
take for granted   take into account   take seriously   track

Will we always pay to play? That's the question the music industry is asking itself. And it's a question which is worth **(1)** ________________ because billions of dollars are at stake. Will people always be willing to pay money to own song **(2)** ________________, or is illegal **(3)** ________________ going to become the norm? Are people starting to **(4)** ________________ the idea that music should be free? When making decisions about its future, the music industry has to **(5)** ________________ the fact that online services which **(6)** ________________ music to a variety of devices in return for a monthly fee are the new reality. People who **(7)** ________________ to such a service don't own the music, yet they can listen to it on demand, so they no longer need to buy it. Actually, the idea that we should be able to "own" music is only around 100 years old. Before then, all music was live and musicians made money from performing, as well as selling the **(8)** ________________ to sheet music. Of course **(9)** ________________ of music, books, or any other intellectual material is wrong, but these industries have to figure out how to exist within the new world of technology. Do they **(10)** ________________ to make the necessary changes?

8–10 correct: I can use idiomatic expressions with *take* and talk about sharing music.
0–7 correct: Look again at Sections 1 and 6 on pages 130, 131, and 134. **SCORE:** /10

2 GRAMMAR

Cross out the incorrect word in each sentence and write the correct word above it. (10 points)

1. Unless I know who a street performer was, I wouldn't give him money.
2. It was Nietzsche he said that without music, life would be a mistake.
3. Who I don't understand is why buying tracks online is so expensive.
4. Suppose it is cheaper to buy music online—would you still download it illegally?
5. Don't you wish you have as much musical talent as your brother?
6. The reason for I don't like his music is that his lyrics are very violent.
7. I wouldn't be a musician these days if you pay me a million dollars!
8. It is her use of the media what I most admire about Victoria Beckham.
9. I think it's time musicians realize that they're going to have to tour more.
10. It was the rapper Keith Cowboy which coined the phrase "hip-hop."

8–10 correct: I can use the past for unreal situations, and cleft sentences.
0–7 correct: Look again at Sections 2 and 4 on pages 131, 132 and 133. **SCORE:** /10

WRITING WORKSHOP

Writing a review

A Prepare to write a review of an album. Read the assignment and the review. Then write a short answer to each question below.

Assignment: Choose an album that you know well and write a review of about 250 words.

FOREVERLY:

NORAH JONES AND BILLIE JOE ARMSTRONG

The most surprising album of the year may be *Foreverly*, which is a collection of songs from a 1958 Everly Brothers album. The Everly Brothers became famous in the early 1960s for hit pop songs like "Wake Up Little Susie," after starting out as country-folk singers in the 1950s. A whole album of covers of songs from 1958 is unexpected enough, but it is the artists who made this album that create the real surprise. The old country-folk-pop songs are sung by jazz star Norah Jones and punk pop star Billie Joe Armstrong (lead singer of Green Day). The idea for this unusual collaboration apparently began when the two singers met while they were performing with Stevie Wonder.

The album begins with a strong, fast song called "Roving Gambler," but if listeners expect the whole album to be like that track they may be a bit disappointed. Most of the songs are slow country-folk ballads about unhappy events. Unless you are a real fan of folk music, you may feel that the songs begin to sound repetitive about halfway through the album. However, it is the technical perfection of the vocals that make this album worth listening to, and it's probably worth buying at least a couple of the tracks even if you don't like the music enough to buy the whole album.

Review by Owen Manning

1 What is the reviewer's overall opinion of the album?
2 Why does the reviewer say that this album is "surprising"?
3 What does the reviewer like about the album? What does he dislike?
4 After reading the review, are you interested in listening to this album? Why or why not?

B Work in pairs. Read the review again. Then make notes about the review under these headings.

- Adjectives used to describe the album in general or the song tracks on the album
- Background information (the musicians, the origin of the ideas for the album, the origin of the tracks)
- The reviewer's opinion (good points and bad points, and whether he likes or doesn't like the album in general)

C Choose a different album to review and make notes under the headings.

- Adjectives for describing the album or elements of the album (vocals, backup musicians, etc.)
- Background information (the musicians, the origin of the ideas for the album or the tracks, etc.)
- Your recommendation (reasons why you like or don't like the album, and how many stars you would give it)

D Write your review. Post it on the classroom wall. Then read your classmates' reviews. Say whether you will listen to any of the albums based on the reviews.

HOW ARE YOU DOING?

- ◯ I have included interesting or important background information.
- ◯ I have used adjectives to make my review clearer and more interesting.
- ◯ I have mentioned several specific things that I like or don't like about the album.

UNIT 12 DOWN TO EARTH

IN THIS UNIT YOU

- learn language to talk about geology and natural phenomena
- listen to a conversation about the structure of the Earth
- write an editorial about climate change
- read about a town facing major environmental changes
- talk about mysterious phenomena
- learn about maximizing your potential
- watch a video about polar research

LISTENING

difficult situations

In real life, outside the classroom, what things can make it difficult to understand what someone is saying?

WRITING

an editorial

What newspapers and/or magazines do you read? Do they usually include a short article where the editor gives an opinion? Why do some newspapers/magazines include this?

LIFE SKILLS

WORK & CAREER

maximizing your potential Many people never achieve their full potential. Suggest reasons why that might be the case.

A Work in pairs. Look at the extreme environments where people live. Discuss which place you think is the hardest to survive in.

Danakil Desert, Ethiopia, one of the hottest places on Earth (temperatures above 49°C)

Oymyakon, Russia, coldest permanently inhabited location (record low of -67.7°C)

La Rinconada, Peru, highest permanently inhabited location (5,100 m above sea level)

Mawsynram, India, wettest place on Earth (annual rainfall 11,872 mm)

B Work in pairs. Discuss the questions.

1. What is life like for people who live in the environments in the pictures? What difficulties do they face?
2. What might be some benefits of living in places like the ones in the pictures?
3. What extreme environments, if any, would you like to visit? Why?

1 GRAMMAR: participle clauses

A LANGUAGE IN CONTEXT Read the homepage for Death Valley Tours. Why might tourists visit this unusual destination?

Welcome | Tours | Rates | FAQs | Contact Us

DEATH VALLEY TOURS

Inhabited by the Timbisha Shoshone Tribe for the last 1,000 years, Death Valley is the hottest, driest location in North America. Roasting under temperatures that can reach 57°C, Death Valley may not be most people's first choice as a holiday destination! Named "Death Valley" by prospectors during the California Gold Rush, it actually has amazing scenery and some fascinating history, like the ghost town of Rhyolite. Housing up to 5,000 people around 1908, Rhyolite had been abandoned by 1920. Some of the buildings still stand, having been preserved by the desert climate.

Having ventured into the desert, photographers will want to capture the vistas, from Dante's View at 1,670 meters above sea level down to the desert floor at 86 meters below sea level. Amateur geologists can explore the history of the land, with our experienced nature guides to explain the rock formations. Having faced one of the harshest environments that nature can throw at you, you're bound to come back with stories to tell! Email or call our representative for more information.

NOTICE!

Which is the main clause in the first sentence? What is the purpose of the other clause?

B ANALYZE Read the homepage in Exercise A again.

Form & Function Choose the correct options to complete the first rule. Then complete the table with examples from the homepage.

Present participle clauses are used like relative clauses in the *active / passive* voice:
Roasting under temperatures that can reach 57° C, Death Valley is …
(1) ______________________________, …

Past participle clauses are used like relative clauses in the *active / passive* voice:
Inhabited by the Timbisha Shoshone Tribe for the last 1,000 years, Death Valley is …
(2) ______________________________, …

Present perfect participle clauses are used to describe *causes and effects / present examples*, in either the active or passive voice:
Some of the buildings still stand, having been preserved by the desert climate.
(3) ______________________________, …
(4) ______________________________, …

C PRACTICE Rewrite each sentence using a participle clause.

1 The prospectors, who were looking for gold, found nothing but rocks.
____

2 Rhyolite, which was founded in 1905, was once a thriving town.
____

3 Once you have visited Death Valley, you will never look at the desert in the same way again.
____

4 Death Valley National Park, which is located on the border between California and Nevada, was created in 1994.
____

5 Because I had heard how hot it was in Death Valley, I took plenty of water.
____

WATCH OUT!

✗ Having booked the tour, the thought of Death Valley started to make me nervous.

✓ Having booked the tour, I started to get nervous at the thought of Death Valley.

D NOW YOU DO IT Work in groups. Write a travel ad to convince people to visit an area that you know about. Use participle clauses where appropriate.

Located conveniently close to the city, this mountain region is perfect for a short break.

2 LISTENING: difficult situations page 123

When background noise obscures what someone says, you have to decide how important the missing information is. It is often possible to ignore something that isn't particularly important. If it's important, you may be able to infer the information from context, or ask for repetition or clarification.

A Work in groups. List situations where background noises could make it difficult to understand people. Discuss how to cope with this.

B **2.27** Listen to parts of a conversation about plate tectonics. Guess what information might be missing from the statements.

1 Yeah, it was pretty ________________.
2 And there are, let's see, ________________ major ways.
3 OK, you were there for ________________ on plate tectonics, right?
4 Oh, like a ________________, right?
5 And then there's erosion, like when mountains get worn down by ________________ …

C **2.28** Listen to the complete conversation and check your answers for Exercise B. Then check the sentences the listener uses to ask for repetition or clarification.

- ☐ Sorry, how many?
- ☐ Wait, what did you say?
- ☐ Didn't get that.
- ☐ Hang on, I didn't catch that.
- ☐ Sorry, could you repeat that?
- ☐ Just a second. Was that water?

D **VOCABULARY: GEOLOGY** Label the picture with the words and phrases from the box.

collide crust drift apart earthquake erosion mountain range plate volcano

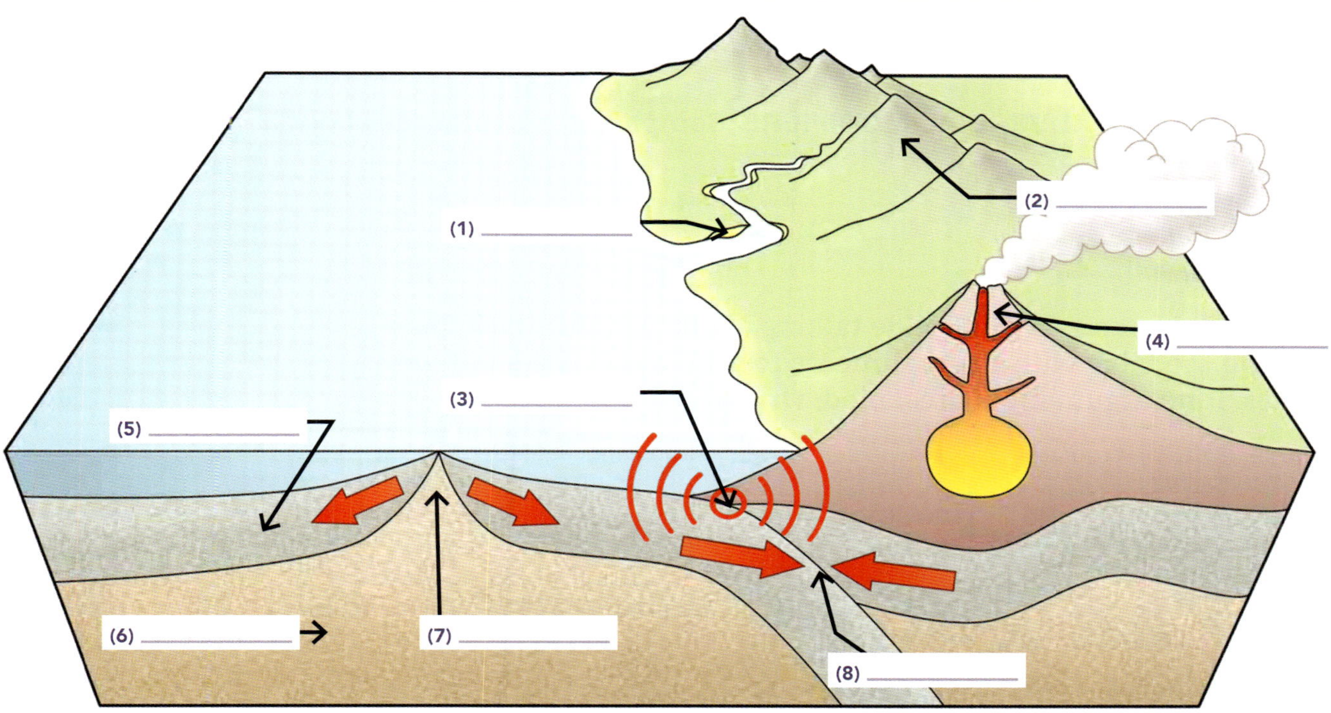

E **VOCABULARY: GEOLOGY** Work in pairs. What can happen when the Earth's plates drift apart or collide? What examples of the phenomena do you know of?

3 SPEAKING: talking about a mysterious phenomenon

A Read the travel blog. What explanation for the moving stones does the writer think is most likely?

Kate and Dan's Desert Adventure

May 3

On our third day, we took a trip to photograph Racetrack Playa in Death Valley. What an incredibly beautiful place! To be there is like being on the surface of another planet or something. It's completely flat and so totally dry that the mud is cracked, like the skin of an enormous lizard. But what's most amazing about the Racetrack Playa is its mysterious moving stones. That's right—moving stones. These rocks range in size from slightly smaller than my fist to rocks so big I couldn't wrap my arms around them. And … they move. They slide. They leave long tracks across the land. What's especially interesting is that no one knows how they move! No one has ever seen it happen. I think the only explanation that is somewhat believable is that people are moving them, perhaps as a trick or a joke. They could come out at night to move the rocks, and disappear by morning. It's great publicity, in any case.

Leave a comment

B VOCABULARY: ADVERBIAL MODIFIERS Read the text again and underline the adverbial modifiers from the table. Then write each word from the box under the adverbial modifier it could appear with.

beautiful believable different difficult dry expensive flat
good important interesting new smaller surprising wrong

incredibly	completely	totally	slightly	especially	somewhat

C VOCABULARY: ADVERBIAL MODIFIERS Complete the sentences about a place you know.

1 … is an incredibly … place.
2 It is completely …
3 It is slightly … than …
4 What's especially … is that …
5 In addition, it is totally …
6 However, it is also somewhat …

D 2.29 Listen to a tour guide talking about the Racetrack Playa. Complete the table with the arguments for and against the different theories. If no argument is presented, write *None*.

Theory	Arguments for	Arguments against
1 supernatural		
2 wind		
3 ice		
4 animals		
5 people		

E **Independent Speaking** Choose two or three of the theories of how the rocks move. (You can also propose your own theory.) In pairs, talk about which theory you think is the most likely, and explain why.

4 GRAMMAR: impersonal passive in the past

A LANGUAGE IN CONTEXT **Read the textbook excerpt about continental drift and plate tectonics. How have ideas about the formation of mountains changed?**

Plate tectonic theory

In plate tectonic theory, the Earth's crust is considered to be composed of large, separate plates. These plates are known to have formed long ago, creating one large supercontinent called Pangaea (see figure 1). The movement of the plates is thought to have created today's continents. These plates are still moving at a rate of about two to ten centimeters per year—the rate at which your fingernails grow.

The theory has its roots in the work of Alfred Wegener, who described the movements of the continents (*continental drift*) in 1915. At the time, the Earth's crust was believed by many to be solid and contracting. Mountains were said to have been the last parts to contract, which was why they were so high. Continental drift was assumed to be impossible, until mounting evidence proved otherwise. Mountains, earthquakes, volcanoes and other geological phenomena are now known to have been the result of the movement of tectonic plates.

NOTICE!

In the first two sentences, find two examples of the passive. What form follows each one? Which one refers to an event that happened in the past?

B ANALYZE **Read the excerpt in Exercise A again.**

Form **Complete the table with examples from the text.**

Structure	Example
subject + impersonal passive + perfect infinitive	These plates are known to have formed long ago, … The movement of the plates **(1)** ______________ today's continents. Mountains **(2)** ______________ the last parts to contract. These geological phenomena **(3)** ______________ the result of …
subject + impersonal passive + infinitive	The Earth's crust is considered to be composed of large plates.

WATCH OUT!

✗ Soccer is believed by some to originate in China.

✓ Soccer is believed by some to have originated in China

Function **Choose the correct option to complete the rule.**

We can use an impersonal passive with a perfect infinitive when we refer to events and situations that happened *before / after* the impersonal verb.

The movement of the plates is thought ***to have created*** *today's continents.*

Mountains were said ***to have been*** *the last parts to contract.*

Compare this to when events happen at the same time as the impersonal verb:

The Earth's crust is considered ***to be composed*** *of large plates.*

At the time, the Earth's crust was believed by many ***to be solid and contracting****.*

C PRACTICE **Rewrite each sentence using an impersonal passive.**

1. People estimate the Earth formed 4.5 billion years ago.
   The Earth ______________________________.
2. People understand that Abraham Ortelius first suggested continental drift in 1596.
   Abraham Ortelius ______________________________.
3. It is thought that the continents once formed one land mass.
   The continents ______________________________.

D NOW YOU DO IT **Work in pairs. You are a TV news announcer reporting on one of these events. Write a short report, using the impersonal passive where appropriate. Then present your report to the class.**

- a recent volcanic eruption
- a recent earthquake
- another recent natural disaster

5 PRONUNCIATION: stress shifts in parts of speech

A 2.30 **Listen to the pairs of words. Notice that the underlined stressed syllable of each word in a pair is different.**

geology—geological
photograph—photographer
reality—realistic
possible—possibility
active—activity
appreciate—appreciation
expect—expectation
progress—progressive
resident—residential

B 2.31 **Listen and practice the sentences. Pay attention to syllable stress. Then practice the sentences with a partner.**

1 That photographer takes photographs of interesting geological formations.
2 We appreciate the residents' progressive attitude.
3 Today I expect to make slightly better progress than yesterday.
4 Is it possible for us to show her our appreciation?

6 READING: a travel memoir

A Read the excerpts from Peter Hessler's memoir *River Town*, about his time living in China in 1998–1999. Do you think he supported or opposed the construction of the Three Gorges Dam (completed in 2008)?

RIVER TOWN

Fuling after the dam was built

Fuling before the dam was built

[1]In town I knew exactly where the waterline of the new Yangtze would be, because there were signs that marked its future rise. One was in the old part of Fuling, painted in red on the side of a snack shop. There was another in downtown's Mid-Mountain Road, which was the second big street above the docks.

[2]Both of these signs said the same thing in huge red numbers: "177 m." This figure represented the future water level of the reservoir, which at its maximum could be filled to an elevation of 177 meters (581 feet) above sea level. There were red signs like this in all of the Yangtze settlements, and heading downstream the numbers marched steadily up the hillsides, until at last you came to low-lying towns like Wushan, where the signs were so far above the city that nothing would be left once the dam reached full capacity in 2009.

...

[3]Sometimes when I was in town I'd stop and watch the 177-meter signs for a few minutes on an average morning. Outside the snack shop, children would be playing, and stick-stick soldiers would be carrying loads up the steps, and the woman who owned the shop would have a yellow pot of bean curd steaming in her doorway. On Mid-Mountain Road there would be unemployed laborers standing with bow saws and paintbrushes, looking for work, and shoeshine men and small-time entrepreneurs would have their stands set up next to the sign. Everywhere I looked, it was typical, everyday life; and yet in a decade all of it would be below the level of the new reservoir.

[4]And by walking downhill I could see just how much more of the city would be affected: the majority of the old town with its buildings of tile and wood, and the entire shop district of Mid-Mountain Road and Riverside Road. They were lively parts of the city, and the people always seemed too busy to look twice at those signs. The river wasn't scheduled to start rising until 2003, which for the residents of Fuling was a long time away. They had other things to worry about.

River Town: Two years on the Yangtze

B Choose T (true) or F (false).

1 The 177-meter signs showed how high the water level was in the past. T / F
2 The town of Fuling would one day be completely underwater. T / F
3 The residents of Fuling were angry about the changes. T / F

C Work in pairs. Discuss the questions.

1 Why did Hessler describe the life of the residents of Fuling in such detail?
2 Why didn't the residents of Fuling pay more attention to the 177-meter signs?
3 What would be the reaction in your hometown if a similar dam were built there?

7 WRITING: an editorial

An editorial is a newspaper article in which an editor gives an opinion on an issue in the news. There is usually a description of the general situation, followed by a rejection of opposing arguments before the presentation of the main argument. Each paragraph often begins with a strong topic sentence.

A Read the editorial about the Three Gorges Dam. Then write the numbers of three topic sentences from the list in the appropriate places in the editorial.

1 However, the dam's advantages outweigh the harm it has caused.
2 The dam project cost around 30 billion U.S. dollars, which was less than original estimates.
3 The Three Gorges Dam is one of the largest engineering projects ever undertaken.
4 There was plenty of controversy surrounding the construction of the dam.
5 Today, the dam is considered to be a more important landmark than the Great Wall of China.

The Three Gorges Dam as an Example for the Future

☐ [1]Spanning the Yangtze River in China, it is currently the largest electricity-generating plant in the world. Construction on the dam began in 1994, with the main body of the dam being finished in 2006. The final electric generator was completed in 2008.

☐ [2]First of all, the water level flooded much of the surrounding area, and well over one million people are thought to have been displaced. Secondly, important archaeological sites were permanently covered by the water. Some pieces were removed, but many more could not be. Animals also lost their homes. The endangered Siberian crane used to winter in that area, and the Yangtze River dolphin is now thought to have been made extinct. Further environmental problems are perhaps still being caused. However, if our species is to survive, these are consequences we must learn to accept as an inevitable part of our large-scale engineering of our environment.

☐ [3]As home to one-quarter of the world's population, China has enormous energy needs, and clearly, a dependence on fossil fuels to meet all of those needs would be short-sighted. To use hydroelectric power instead of coal, oil, or gas also greatly reduces air pollution that contributes to global warming. Furthermore, the dam is being used to control flooding, which used to threaten major cities built along the Yangtze. People can use technology and intelligence to overcome environmental problems. However, in order to do this, they have to be able to generate the energy they need. I hope other countries learn from China's example and are not afraid to make large, or even enormous, changes to the Earth in order for our condition to be improved.

B Work in pairs. Discuss the questions.

1 Is the writer for or against the Three Gorges Dam?
2 What is the purpose of each paragraph?

C Choose one of the points of view. Write a three-paragraph editorial.

1 Climate change will only be solved by the development of technology.
2 Technology will never provide solutions to the challenges of climate change.

lifeSkills

MAXIMIZING YOUR POTENTIAL

- Understand the difference between hard skills and soft skills and the importance of each.
- Assess your soft skills, and decide which areas you need to improve.
- Consider practical ways in which you can continue to develop your life skills.

A 2.32 **Listen to a conversation between a person looking for a job and a job counselor. What three areas help contribute to an outstanding résumé?**

B **Work in pairs. Listen again. Then discuss the questions with your partner.**

1 At the beginning of the conversation, does Noel think he stands a good chance of getting a job? Why or why not?
2 Why does the counselor think Noel's part-time jobs are relevant to his career?
3 What is the difference between hard and soft skills?

C **Make a list of your hard skills. Compare lists with a partner. Decide which ones you expect to be most important in your career in the future.**

D **First, complete the table with the labels. Add one more skill to each category. Then, reflect on your own soft skills and write *G* (good), *A* (average), or *NI* (need to improve) next to each skill in the Assessment column of the table.**

Critical thinking   Information literacy   Interpersonal

Soft skill area	Skill	Assessment
(1) ________ skills	Understanding decision-making styles	
	Building communities	
	Giving and receiving feedback	
(2) ________ skills	Evaluating claims and explanations	
	Identifying bias	
	Organizing an argument	
(3) ________ skills	Evaluating internet source reliability	
	Protecting digital privacy	
	Recognizing and avoiding plagiarism	

E Work in groups. Add another two skills to the table. Brainstorm ideas for practical steps you could take to develop each of the soft skills listed. Complete the table with your favorite idea for each skill.

Soft skill	Ideas for development
Understanding decision-making styles	Analyze how decisions are made in groups you are involved in (e.g., groups, clubs, teams). Suggest ways of improving the decision-making process.
Building communities	Start a social network group with people in the same job or major as yours.
Giving and receiving feedback	
Evaluating claims and explanations	Read and comment on blogs about controversial issues that interest you.
Identifying bias	
Organizing an argument	
Evaluating internet source reliability	
Protecting digital privacy	
Recognizing and avoiding plagiarism	Speak to your boss/tutor about how they want sources to be referenced.

F Work in groups. Discuss how each person's soft skills may be relevant in their future career. Your group may suggest skills you didn't know you had!

G Discuss the questions.

1. What have you learned about maximizing your potential?
2. How exactly are you going to maximize your potential in the future?

REFLECT … How can the skill of maximizing your potential be useful to you in **Study & Learning** and **Self & Society**?

RESEARCH …

Choose one life skill you have studied over the course which particularly interested you. Research advice on developing that life skill. See what at least three different people have to say about it. Do they all agree on the best ways to develop the skill? Think about what makes most sense to you and decide how you're going to further develop that life skill.

Language wrap-up

1 VOCABULARY

A Complete the sentences with the words and phrases from the box. One word or phrase is not used. (6 points)

collided erosion drifted apart earthquake mountain ranges plates volcano

1 The Himalayas are one of the world's most famous ______________.
2 A terrible accident occurred when the two boats ______________.
3 The Grand Canyon was formed by ______________ from the Colorado River.
4 The Earth's ______________ are responsible for continental drift.
5 The ______________ erupted and formed a new island in the ocean.
6 The ______________ was caused by a sudden release of pressure along the tectonic plates.

B Complete the sentences with the words from the box. There may be more than one correct answer. (6 points)

completely especially incredibly slightly totally somewhat

1 A tour to Antarctica is ______________ expensive these days, but I still want to go.
2 The Himalayan mountains are ______________ difficult to climb.
3 The night sky was ______________ dark away from the city lights.
4 Lake Baikal is ______________ deeper than Lake Tanganyika.
5 We were ______________ affected by the beauty of the sunset.
6 I was ______________ surprised by his desire to travel to China.

10–12 correct: I can talk about common geological features and use adverbial modifiers to strengthen or weaken adjectives.
0–9 correct: Look again at Sections 2 and 3 on pages 143 and 144. **SCORE:** /12

2 GRAMMAR

Find and underline 10 mistakes in the text. Write the correct forms. (12 points)

CLIMBING EVEREST

Locate in Nepal, Mount Everest has always fascinated me. Having been climbed smaller mountains, it was my next challenge. Mighty forces are thought to created the Himalayas, forces so powerful that they have pushed Everest up to become the roof of the world. The Yeti is said to have choose Everest as his home. Arrived in Nepal, it was easy to see why; the peak is so high, it is completely lost in the clouds. Anyone could hide out in such a remote place.

Or at least, they could until recently! Over four thousand people are thought have climbed Everest. Loading with gear, amateurs arrive, sometimes up to 200 at once, and try to reach the summit. They are thought to have cause considerable damage to the climbing routes and to have left a huge amount of garbage behind them. Live in the shadow of the mountain, the Nepalese are understandably unhappy about this situation. Know this in advance, I was determined to be a model climber. Bringing only the equipment I knew I would need, I decided to hire a local guide to take me on a route the tourists would never find.

8–10 correct: I can use participle clauses, and impersonal passives in the past.
0–7 correct: Look again at Sections 1 and 4 on pages 142 and 145. **SCORE:** /10

SPEAKING WORKSHOP

Giving a mini-presentation

A 2.33 **Listen to the short presentation. First, decide which of the three topics the speaker is presenting on. Then take notes on her main points. In pairs, compare notes.**

- **A: The English language:** why it's a key element of your future success
- **B: Education:** the need for more language education in schools
- **C: Learning English:** being responsible for your own learning in the future

B Listen again for phrases the speaker uses to link her ideas together. Write a word or short phrase in each blank. Suggest other phrases that can be used.

1 ________, I can see the need to …
2 This ________ that I have to …
3 ________ and foremost, it's important to …
4 What's ________, I'm aware of …
5 ________ that, reading …
6 In a ________ way, listening …
7 To briefly ________, there are …

C Prepare for a short talk on one of the topics below. First, choose a topic you would like to talk about. Then make notes to complete the presentation planner.

- **A: Communication:** how to become a better communicator
- **B: Success:** what it takes to be successful
- **C: Life skills:** how they can help you in many aspects of your life

Presentation planner
Chosen topic: ________
Intro: general statement; relevant personal experience
First main point: ________
Supporting details or reasons: ________
Second main point: ________
Supporting details or reasons: ________
Third main point: ________
Supporting details or reasons: ________
Brief concluding statement

D Present your talk to the class. Then invite the class to ask questions and answer them.

HOW ARE YOU DOING?

- ◯ I presented a clear argument on the topic chosen.
- ◯ I spoke for the whole time, without unnecessary pauses or hesitation.
- ◯ I used good linking phrases to connect my ideas.

Communicative wrap-up
Units 7–8

1 PACK IT UP

A **Work in pairs. Look at the products and discuss the questions.**

- Who buys or uses these products? What for, and in which situations?
- Does using these products cause any harm to the environment? If so, how?

B **With your partner, choose one of the products and decide how it could be produced, packaged, or used in a more environmentally friendly manner. Then compare ideas with another pair.**

2 ADVERB TIC-TAC-TOE

Work in pairs. Follow the instructions to play the game.

- Decide who is **X** and who is **O**. Flip a coin to decide who starts. Start with Game 1.
- When it's your turn, choose a square. Form a grammatically correct sentence with the phrase in the square. If your sentence is correct, write **X** or **O** on that square. If your sentence is wrong, don't write anything.
- Continue until someone gets three **X**'s or **O**'s across, down, or diagonally.
- Repeat with Game 2.

Examples:
before coming: "I always have a cup of coffee before coming to class."
Being concerned: "Being concerned about the environment, Sarah started recycling more."

GAME 1

before cooking	since learning	wanting
not being	having read about	since realizing
having talked to	while eating	before choosing

GAME 2

having done	after having	being worried about
when watching	not wanting	after finishing
having seen	while driving	hoping

3 POINTS OF VIEW

Work in groups. A donor is offering your school one work of art. Discuss which one you prefer and why.

4 A GALLERY TOUR

A Work in pairs. Prepare a short talk about one work of art on this page. Practice your talk together, giving half the talk each.

B With your partner, find another pair that chose a different work of art for their talk. Take turns giving your talks.

SCORE YOURSELF!

Score 1–5 for the items below. Score 5 for things that are easy and 1 for things that are difficult.

I can talk about consumer products and their environmental impact.	5	4	3	2	1
I can express time and cause-effect relationships.	5	4	3	2	1
I can describe different styles of art and give opinions on them.	5	4	3	2	1
I can prepare and present a talk about a work of art.	5	4	3	2	1

If you gave yourself 1 or 2 for any of the statements, look at Units 7 and 8 again.

Communicative wrap-up Units 9–10

1 BRAIN POWER

A Work in pairs. Follow the instructions to take the quiz.

- Work together to answer the quiz questions as quickly as possible. Make sure you agree on the answers.
- Write each answer in your notebook.
- Raise your hands when you have finished.
- The pair that answers all the questions correctly first wins.

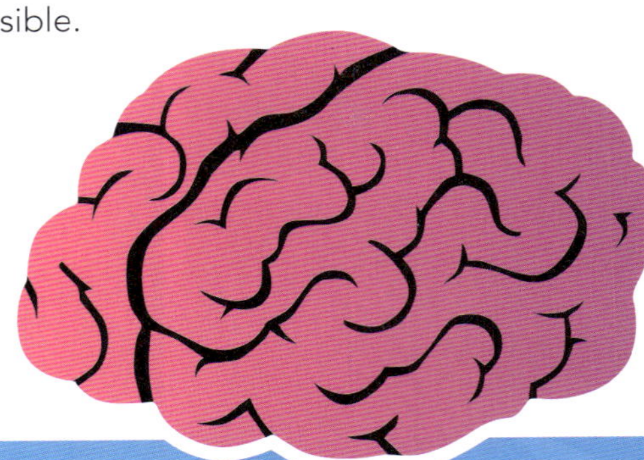

BRAINPOWER

LITERACY

1. **Write what this says:** You can raed tihs wouthit a porbelm bcuseae we do not raed ervey lteter by itslef, but the wrod as a wlohe.

2. **What is the meaning of this proverb?** Silence is foolish if we are wise, but wise if we are foolish. —Charles Caleb Colton

3. **What is the relationship between this sentence and the English alphabet?** The quick brown fox jumps over the lazy dog.

NUMERACY

1. **Is 2 a prime number?**

2. **A car left one town at 6:18 a.m. and arrived at another town 180 miles away at 10:03 a.m. How fast was it traveling?**
   a) 36 mph b) 48 mph
   c) 56 mph d) 65 mph

3. **56/7 = ? – 5**

SPATIAL/VISUAL ABILITY

1. **What is this?**

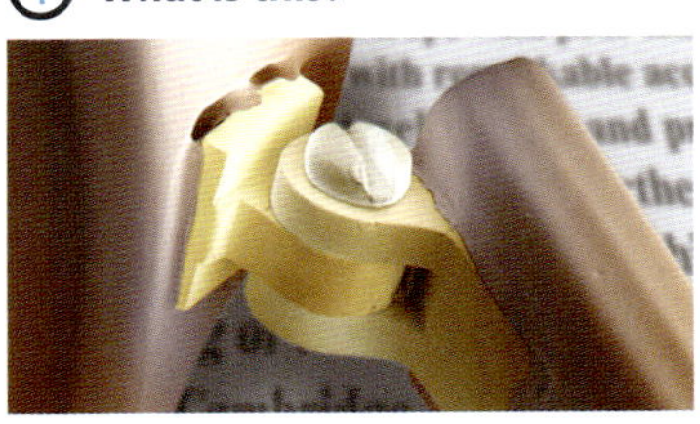

2. **Here are three views of the same cube. Which symbol goes on the blank side of the cube?**

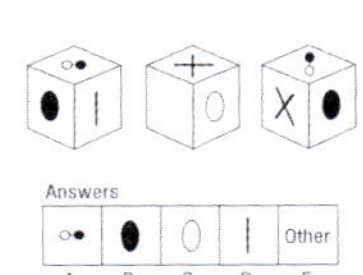

3. **Are the horizontal lines parallel?**
   a) Yes b) No

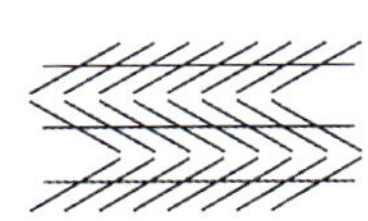

LOGIC

1. Which is heavier, a pound of feathers or a pound of rocks?

2. How can you throw a ball as hard as you can and have it come back to you even if it doesn't bounce off anything? The ball is not attached to anything, and there is no one to throw it back to you.

3. A man who lives on the 10th floor takes the elevator down to the 1st floor every day and goes to work. When he comes home, if there are other people in the elevator, he goes directly to his floor. If not, he goes to the 7th floor and walks up three floors to his apartment. Why?

B Discuss the questions as a class.

1 Which category was the easiest? Which was the most difficult?
2 How can games or quizzes like this be useful?

2 STATE YOUR CASE

Work in groups. Discuss whether you agree or disagree with these statements about media use.

1 People who invent myths or fake news stories on the internet are just engaging in a little fun. The stories are harmless.
2 *Phishing*, which is obtaining information dishonestly, is soon going to be a disappearing crime because people are becoming less gullible.
3 Spending lots of time on the internet has a negative effect on people's ability to socialize and to engage in open-ended, creative thinking.

3 FACE OFF

Work in pairs. Choose a situation and prepare a role-play. Practice your conversation. Then act it out for the class.

SITUATION 1

STUDENT A: Your friends talked you into going on a date with a person who you didn't know. The date wasn't perfect, but you think the person is attractive and that a second date would go better than the first one. You would like to spend some more time with the person, but you're having a hard time getting him/her to accept your invitation for another date.

STUDENT B: You agreed to go on a date with a friend of some of your friends. You didn't have much fun because your date spent most of the time talking about himself/herself. He/She seems to waste a lot of time playing games and debunking phony internet reports. Who cares? The situation is a little embarrassing because the person is trying to convince you to go out again, and you don't want to be too rude.

SITUATION 2

STUDENT A: You have just received a notice from your cell phone provider that they had a lottery with all the names of their customers and that you have won a car. You have called the number provided in the text message from the provider and confirmed that the recorded message is valid. This was verified by the fact that the phone was answered by your service provider. Now you have to send your address and let them know when you will be home. They will bring you the car and the papers to sign.

STUDENT B: Your friend was informed that he/she had won a car in a cell phone provider's lottery. You are certain that this is a hoax. You can't disprove it, but you feel that your friend is a gullible person who has a hard time recognizing dishonesty. You want your friend to think more carefully about what could happen if a person gives out information like their home address and when they are and are not home.

SCORE YOURSELF!
Score 1–5 for the items below. Score 5 for things that are easy and 1 for things that are difficult.

I can give explanations for stated problems.	5	4	3	2	1
I can give opinions on different uses of media.	5	4	3	2	1
I can prepare and sustain an argument.	5	4	3	2	1

If you gave yourself 1 or 2 for any of the statements, look at Units 9 and 10 again.

Communicative wrap-up Units 11–12

1 SURVIVING IN THE WILD

A You are going on a reality TV show that involves living in one of these remote areas for a year. Make notes on what living in these places would be like and which you would prefer.

B You can take these items with you. Write down which item you would take in each category.

one song: ____________________ one luxury item: ____________________
one book: ____________________ one person: ____________________

C Work in pairs. Take turns telling your partner your ideas. Ask each other questions to find out more.

The place I would most like to live in is …
I wouldn't want to live in … unless …
The song I'd take would be …
The person I'd take with me would be …

2 ORGANIZING A FUND-RAISING CONCERT

A Work in small groups. You are organizing a concert to help victims of a natural disaster. Decide which musician/band from each category below to invite.

A: *Suppose we invited Music Unchained? They're fairly unknown, but what's good about them is that they play a variety of different types of music.*
B: *Good idea. And what if we invited The Glamorones? Would they come? They're known to have helped with causes like this in the past.*

Invite a musician/band that …

- is known to have supported good causes
- is fairly unknown (not world-famous)
- is especially popular in your country
- can appeal to a broad range of people

B As a group, present your ideas to the class. Each member of the group should participate. Explain who you have chosen and why.

C As a class, vote on which group's concert would appeal to the most people.

3 WHAT DO YOU KNOW?

Work in small groups. Follow the instructions to play the game.

- Choose one person to be the "monitor" and check the answers and rules.
- Each player except the monitor needs a coin, a watch, and a marker.
- Place all the markers on START and choose someone to go first. The first player flips the coin. If it lands on "heads," the player moves forward two spaces. If it lands on "tails," the player moves forward one space.
- Players take turns flipping the coin, moving their markers, and following the instructions in each square.
- Each player has one minute to complete his or her turn. The monitor says if the answer is correct or incorrect. The first player to land on FINISH is the winner.

START →	1 End of turn. →	2 Explain what the copyright of a piece of music is. ✓ forward 1 ✗ back 1 →	3 End of turn. →	4 Explain what take into account means. ✓ forward 2 ✗ back 1 ↓
9 End of turn. ↓	8 Explain what a busker is. ✓ forward 1 ✗ back 2 ←	7 What is especially interesting about the rocks at Racetrack Playa? ✓ forward 2 ✗ back 1 ←	6 End of turn. ←	5 Today's continents are known to be moving … how fast? ✓ forward 1 ✗ back 2 ←
10 Explain what music piracy is. ✓ forward 2 ✗ back 1 →	11 Explain what it means if you take something for granted. ✓ forward 2 ✗ back 2 →	12 End of turn. →	13 End of turn. →	14 Explain what happens when you stream music. ✓ forward 1 ✗ back 2 ↓
19 Explain how today's continents are thought to have been formed. ✓ forward 1 ✗ back 2 ↓	18 End of turn. ←	17 End of turn. ←	16 Name two songs with a person's name in the title. ✓ forward 2 ✗ back 1 ←	15 End of turn. ←
20 What is another word for a song on an album? ✓ forward 2 ✗ back 2 →	21 End of turn. →	22 End of turn. →	23 Name at least two natural phenomena that are known to be caused by the movement of continental plates. forward 2 back 1 →	24 End of turn. ↓
FINISH	28 What do Bob Dylan, Paul McCartney, and Tracy Chapman have in common? ✓ forward 1 ✗ back 2 ←	27 What instrument does Joshua Bell play? forward 2 back 3 ←	26 End of turn. ←	25 What was the name of the band Michael Jackson was in when he was a child? ✓ forward 1 ✗ back 1 ←

SCORE YOURSELF!

Score 1–5 for the items below. Score 5 for things that are easy and 1 for things that are difficult.

I can talk about facts related to music and the Earth.	5	4	3	2	1
I can talk about unreal or hypothetical situations.	5	4	3	2	1
I can discuss the pros and cons of different options.	5	4	3	2	1

If you gave yourself 1 or 2 for any of the statements, look at Units 11 and 12 again.

Grammar reference

UNIT 7

REDUCED ADVERB TIME CLAUSES

Function **Clauses can be reduced when the subject is the same in both clauses.**

Form **Rule for reducing the time clause**	**Full adverb time clause example**	**Reduced adverb time clause example**
If the clause is in the present progressive, delete the subject and the verb *be*.	*When you are trying to save money, do you change your shopping habits?*	*When trying to save money, do you change your shopping habits?*
If the clause is not in the present progressive, delete the subject and change the verb to the *–ing* form.	*I always wash food containers before I put them in the recycling bin.*	*I always wash food containers before putting them in the recycling bin.*

1 Check the sentences that can use a reduced adverb time clause.

1 I understood more about the health risks of sugar after I read the article. ☐
2 Before he takes the exam on Monday, Jack will spend Sunday reviewing his notes from last term. ☐
3 While Sophie was visiting San Francisco, her brother looked after her cat. ☐

2 Rewrite the sentences with reduced adverb time clauses where possible.

1 Since Victoria planted a vegetable garden, she has not bought many vegetables from the supermarket.
____
2 After she moved to Colorado, Beth joined a number of new social groups.
____
3 Most consumers research different smartphones when they decide what model to buy.
____

REDUCED ADVERB CAUSE-EFFECT CLAUSES

Rule for reducing the cause-effect clause	**Full adverb cause-effect clause example**	**Reduced adverb cause-effect clause example**
Delete the subject and the word that signals cause (e.g., *since*, *because*). Change the verb to the *–ing* form.	*Because she doesn't believe the advertising claims about "healthy" snack bars, she never buys them.*	*Not believing the advertising claims about "healthy" snack bars, she never buys them.*
Note that for perfect tense verbs, you change the auxiliary verb (e.g., *have*, *had*) not the main verb.	*Because I've reduced the amount of meat in my diet, I'm spending less on food these days.*	*Having reduced the amount of meat in my diet, I'm spending less on food these days.*

1 Complete the sentences with reduced adverb cause-effect clauses.

1 We had eaten there before, so we knew what type of food to expect.
_______ eaten there before, we knew what type of food to expect.
2 Because she's half Turkish, Carolina's the perfect person to show us around Istanbul.
_______ half Turkish, Carolina's the perfect person to show us around Istanbul.
3 Since we didn't want to wait for a bus, we took a taxi.
Not _______ to wait for a bus, we took a taxi.

2 Complete the second sentence in each pair with a reduced adverb cause-effect clause so that they are similar in meaning.

1 Because the band is really popular, they always sell lots of tickets to their concerts.
_______________, the band always sell lots of tickets to their concerts.
2 Since it is a coastal town, New Orleans is susceptible to flooding when there is heavy rain.
_______________, New Orleans is susceptible to flooding when there is heavy rain.
3 I almost didn't recognize David at first because I hadn't seen him for so many years.
_______________, I almost didn't recognize him at first.

UNIT 8

INVERTED CONDITIONALS

Function **Inverted conditionals are more formal than standard conditionals. They tend to occur more in writing than in speaking.**

Form

	Change required	Standard conditional examples	Inverted conditional examples
Present	Change *if* to *should*.	*If you want to see surrealist paintings, visit MoMA.* *If you don't wish to participate in the survey, please check this box.*	*Should you want to see surrealist paintings, visit MoMA.* *Should you not wish to participate in the survey, please check this box.*
Past	Remove *if* and change the order of the subject and the auxiliary verb.	*If you had worn gloves, you wouldn't have burned your hand.* *If you hadn't come so late, you wouldn't have missed the show.*	*Had you worn gloves, you wouldn't have burned your hand.* *Had you not come so late, you wouldn't have missed the show.*

1 Choose the correct option to complete the sentences.

1 Should you *decide* / *decided* to participate as a volunteer, please inform us via email.
2 *Had* / *Should* you stuck to your budget, you would have been able to afford a new car.
3 They would have understood that breakfast was not included *had* / *should* they read the brochure.

2 Rewrite the sentences as inverted conditionals.

1 If you had read the food labels, you would have noticed the high sugar content.

____

2 If you feel dissatisfied with the service, please write to our customer service department.

____

3 More people would have attended the play if they'd known about it.

____

ADJECTIVE PHRASE + INDIRECT QUESTION

Function **We use indirect questions with adjective phrases when we are considering something and don't have (or expect) a definite answer.**

Form	**Examples**
It + *be* + adjective (*for* + indirect object) + infinitive – indirect question (with *what, where, who, why, when, how, if/whether*)	*It will be interesting to see what happens.* *It's hard for him to think about where he will go after he graduates.*

1 There is one missing word in each sentence. Rewrite the sentences correctly.

1 It would fun to try an online dating site where you can't see people's photographs.

____

2 It's important think about whether you can afford something before you buy it.

____

3 It's difficult to know Mike will visit. He always comes without telling us.

____

2 Use the prompts to form sentences with adjective phrases and indirect questions.

1 would / useful / us / consider / how / the company / could reduce expenses

____

2 important / people / find out / why / government / cut / public services

____

3 hard / know / what / weather / be like / later / because / so unpredictable

____

THE SUBJUNCTIVE

Function The subjunctive is used in formal English to emphasize requests, orders, and recommendations.

Use	Form	Examples
With verbs: *ask, demand, insist, propose, recommend, suggest, require*	**Affirmative:** subject + verb + *that* + subject + base form	*We suggest that you wake earlier tomorrow.*
	Negative: subject + negative verb + *that* + subject + base form subject + verb + *that* + subject + *not* + base form	*We didn't insist that he see a doctor.* *We asked that he not smoke inside.*
With adjectives: *recommended, necessary, essential, better/best, important*	**Affirmative:** *It* + *be* + adjective + *that* + subject + base form	*It is best that children spend time outdoors.*
	Negative: *It* + *be* + *not* + adjective + *that* + subject + base form *It* + *be* + adjective + *that* + subject + *not* + base form	*It isn't necessary that they attend.* *It is recommended that you not drink coffee late at night.*

1 Complete the sentences with three of the words or phrases from the box.

checks in check in not be didn't be bring bringing

1 The airline representative recommended that he __________ at least three hours before departure.
2 The organization's director proposed that cash donations __________ accepted.
3 It is not essential that you __________ food to the party on Friday.

2 Put the words in the correct order to form sentences.

1 that / your / we / ask / you / copies / identity documents / send / of / .

____

2 while / recommended / the island / you / it's / here / explore / that / you're / .

____

3 Sam / yesterday / suggested / guests / not / bring / sleeping bags / that / .

____

ALTERNATIVES TO THE SUBJUNCTIVE

Use	Alternative form	Example
With verbs *insist, demand*	(No alternative: subjunctive only)	*The electric company is demanding that the customer pay immediately.*
With verbs *ask, require*	verb + object + infinitive	*The store requires customers to exchange unwanted items within 30 days.*
With verbs *recommend, suggest, propose*	verb + gerund	*What do you recommend doing in California?*
With adjectives *important, necessary, better/best*	*It* (+ *would*) + *be* + adjective (+ *for* + object) + infinitive	*It's important for you to listen carefully.* *It would be better to rest before your exam.*

1 Choose the correct option to complete the sentences.

1 The position requires candidates *to speak* / *speaking* two European languages.
2 I suggest *taking* / *to take* regular breaks to study more effectively.
3 It's important *discuss* / *to discuss* any problems you may be having with your supervisor.

2 Complete the sentences using the subjunctive form of the verb in parentheses and any other words you need. Then rewrite each sentence using an alternative.

1 Career advisors recommend ____________ a career you enjoy. (*you / follow*)
____

2 The site asks ____________ with a password. (*people / log on*)
____

3 It's necessary ____________ the tickets early to avoid disappointment. (*people / book*)
____

UNIT 10

INVERSION WITH NEGATIVE EXPRESSIONS

Function **We use inversions after negative adverbs and adverbial phrases for emphasis. They are formal structures that tend to appear more in writing than in speech.**

Form	Use	Examples
Negative adverb/ adverb phrase + auxiliary verb + subject	Phrases referring to time	*Barely had she left the house* ***when*** *it started to rain.* *Hardly had he finished eating breakfast* ***when*** *his wife called.* *No sooner do I buy a new phone* ***than*** *a newer model arrives.* *Scarcely had they opened the door* ***when*** *the alarm went off.*
	Phrases with *only*	*Only when you read the biography do you understand him.* *Not only did we take the bus tour, but we also visited three museums.*
	Other negative adverbs/ adverbial phrases	*Little do we realize how much influence our teachers have.* *Never have I seen such beautiful portraits.* *Rarely did I go to such an expensive restaurant.* *Seldom had I seen so many people in one room.* *Under no circumstances can students retake the exam.*

1 Complete the sentences with the words and phrases from the box.

but did hardly not only only when

1 ________ had he stepped outside ________ it started to rain.
2 ________ when people complained ________ the owner of the bar turn down the music.
3 ________ is the castle the largest in Scotland, ________ it is also the oldest.

2 Complete the rewritten sentences using inversion.

1 When I arrived at the theater the movie began immediately.
Hardly ____________ at the theater when the movie began.
2 Elisa is reliable, and she is a good team player.
Not only ____________, but she's also a good team player.
3 This is the most stunning rooftop view I have ever seen.
Never ____________ such a stunning rooftop view.

ELLIPSIS AND SUBSTITUTION

Function **In ellipsis, we omit some words. It is common in spoken English as well as in informal written communication. We use it in situations where the missing words are obvious from the context. In substitution, we use words such as *so* in place of other words and phrases. We use it to avoid repeating ourselves.**

Form	**Examples**	
Ellipsis: missing unstressed words	*(~~I've~~) Been having a hard time recently.* *(~~Do you~~) Know anything about the new job yet?*	
Ellipsis: reduced relative structures	*Someone (~~who is~~) working at the office will answer the phone.*	
Substitution: expressions using *so*	*I meditate every morning, and in doing so, I find I sleep better.* *We suggest you send an email, and when you do so, copy in the team.*	
	Positive	**Negative**
	I think/expect/believe/imagine so. *I guess/suppose/assume/hope so.*	*I don't think/expect/believe/imagine so.* *I guess/suppose/assume/hope not.*

1 Complete the sentences with one word.

1 **A:** Do you know if Jennifer has canceled dinner next week?
B: I hope ____________. I was really looking forward to it.
2 Hanna is moving out soon. When she ____________ so, tell her there are empty boxes in my room.
3 You should follow your passion in life. In doing ____________, you'll be happier.

2 Rewrite the sentences and shorten them using ellipsis and/or substitution.

1 Do you think you could give me a hand with the cooking? Yes, I think I can do that.
____

2 Have you heard about the plans for a new mall?
____

3 The guy who was sitting next to us in the restaurant looked like an old school friend.
____

UNIT 11

PAST TENSE FOR UNREAL SITUATIONS

Form	**Example**
***Suppose / It's time / What if* + subject + past tense verb**	*Suppose you saw your favorite singer in the street, what would you ask her to sing?*
subject + *wish* + subject + past tense verb	*I wish they played concerts at smaller venues.*
***If/Unless* + past tense verb + *would/wouldn't* + verb**	*Unless you were prepared to practice for hours every day, you wouldn't have a chance of becoming a concert pianist.*

1 Complete the sentences with *It's time*, *I wish*, or *Suppose*.

1 ____________ you played in a band, where would you like to perform?
2 ____________ you didn't have to leave after dinner.
3 ____________ everyone made serious changes to their lifestyles to stop climate change.

2 Rewrite the sentences using the words in parentheses.

1 If you held the relevant teaching qualification, you would be able to apply for the job. (*unless*)
____

2 If you wrote a blog each week about a particular topic, what would you choose? (*suppose*)
____

3 Governments should demand bonus cuts for employees at large banks. (*time*)
____

CLEFT SENTENCES

Function **We use cleft sentences to give emphasis to certain information.**

Form	Example
It + *be* + noun + relative clause	***It was*** *Guillaume Apollinaire* ***who*** *first named the Surrealist movement.*
subject + relative clause + *be* + complement	***The reason why*** *many surrealist artists were influenced by Freud* ***is*** *because he had new ideas about dreams and reality.*
What + verb phrase + clause	***What*** *we know* ***is*** *that this painting is extremely valuable.*

1 Complete the cleft sentences with relative pronouns.

1 It was Jack Kerouac ________ said the only truth is music.
2 It was in this park ________ my grandparents first met.
3 The reason ________ we can't go to the concert is because we don't have tickets.

2 Rewrite each sentence as a cleft sentence.

1 Nelson Mandela said, "It always seems impossible until it's done."
It was ____.
2 We went on vacation to Florida last year.
The place ____.
3 They didn't tell me that the 10-km run was on a mountain.
What they ____.

UNIT 12

PARTICIPLE CLAUSES

Function **Present participle clauses are used like relative clauses in the active voice. Past participle clauses are used like relative clauses in the passive voice. Present perfect participle clauses are used to describe causes and effects. They can use the active or passive voice.**

Participle clauses	Example
Present participle clause	*Featuring stunning views over the mountains, the hotel is ideally situated.*
Past participle clause	*Discovered in 1999, the ancient Mayan ruins are of great interest to local historians.*
Present perfect participle clause	*Having researched several cities in Canada, I chose to live in Vancouver.* *Having been buried for thousands of years, the remains were finally discovered.*

1 Complete the sentences using the verbs in parentheses.

1 ________________ recently, the website has had a million hits in the last week. (*relaunch*)
2 ________________ the topic for two years already, I felt confident about starting the new class. (*study*)
3 ________________ a route used for hundreds of years, the road passes many old villages. (*follow*)

2 Rewrite each sentence using a participle clause.

1 The Swiss Alps train offers some of the world's most beautiful views and is good value.
____
2 Rob had taken it for granted he would get the job, so he didn't prepare for the interview.
____
3 Ronnie was impressed by the writer's knowledge of art and decided to buy his book.
____

IMPERSONAL PASSIVE IN THE PAST

Function **We can use a perfect infinitive with the impersonal passive when we refer to events and situations that happened before the impersonal verb.**

Form	Example
Referring to a time before the impersonal verb: subject + impersonal passive + perfect infinitive	*Michael Jackson is considered to have been one of the best pop stars of his generation.*
Referring to the same time as the impersonal verb: subject + impersonal passive + infinitive	*Sumatran tigers are said to be on the verge of extinction. In the Middle Ages, the Earth was thought to be flat.*

1 Complete the sentences with one word.

1 They are believed to have ________ the best team ever in sporting history.
2 The eruption of Mount Tambora is claimed ________ have been the fiercest in history.
3 A man is reported to ________ been arrested for the armed robbery of a jewelry store yesterday.

2 Complete the rewritten sentences using a passive perfect infinitive.

1 They say that album was the most influential of the last 20 years.
That album is ________________ the most influential of the last 20 years.
2 Scientists have proved that the burning of fossil fuels has led to dramatic changes in the global climate.
The burning of fossil fuels is ________________ to dramatic changes in the global climate.
3 Some historians believed that Marco Polo introduced pasta to Italy after traveling to China.
Marco Polo was ________________ pasta to Italy after traveling to China.

Irregular verbs

Infinitive	Past simple	Past participle
be	was/were	been
become	became	become
begin	began	begun
break	broke	broken
bring	brought	brought
build	built	built
buy	bought	bought
catch	caught	caught
choose	chose	chosen
come	came	come
cost	cost	cost
cut	cut	cut
do	did	done
draw	drew	drawn
drink	drank	drunk
drive	drove	driven
eat	ate	eaten
fall	fell	fallen
feed	fed	fed
feel	felt	felt
find	found	found
fly	flew	flown
get	got	got
give	gave	given
go	went	gone
grow	grew	grown
hang	hung	hung
have	had	had
hear	heard	heard
hit	hit	hit
hold	held	held
hurt	hurt	hurt
keep	kept	kept
know	knew	known
leave	left	left
let	let	let
lose	lost	lost
make	made	made
meet	met	met
pay	paid	paid
put	put	put
read	read	read
ride	rode	ridden
ring	rang	rung
rise	rose	risen
run	ran	run
say	said	said
see	saw	seen
sell	sold	sold
send	sent	sent
set	set	set
sing	sang	sung
sit	sat	sat
speak	spoke	spoken
stand	stood	stood
stick	stuck	stuck
take	took	taken
teach	taught	taught
tell	told	told
think	thought	thought
throw	threw	thrown
understand	understood	understood
wake	woke	woken
wear	wore	worn
win	won	won
write	wrote	written

Pronunciation symbols

Vowels

ɪ	did
e	bed, neck
æ	bad, hand
ɒ	box
ʌ	but, mother
ʊ	book, good
ə	banana, computer
iː	feed
ɑː	father
ɔː	tall
uː	boot, food, student
ɜː	shirt, birthday
eɪ	date, table
aɪ	cry, eye
ɔɪ	boy
əʊ	comb, post
aʊ	about, how
ʊə	tour
eə	their
ɪə	here, near

Consonants

p	park, happy
b	back, hobby
t	tea
d	die
k	came, kitchen, quarter
g	game, go
f	face, photographer
v	vegetable
θ	thing, maths
ð	then, that
s	city, summer
z	please, goes
ʃ	she, shop
ʒ	leisure
h	hot, who
tʃ	chicken, watch
dʒ	jacket, orange
m	men
n	sun, know
ŋ	sung, singer
w	week, white
r	rain, writer
l	light, long
j	yes, use, music

NOTES

NOTES

NOTES

NOTES

Macmillan Education
4 Crinan Street
London N1 9XW
A division of Macmillan Publishers Limited

Companies and representatives throughout the world

ISBN 978-0-230-49418-3

Written by Mickey Rogers, Steve Taylore-Knowles and Dorothy E. Zemach.

The authors have asserted their rights to be identified as the authors of this work in accordance with the Copyright, Designs and Patents Act 1988.

This edition published 2015
First edition published 2010

Designed by emc design limited.
Illustrated by Martin Meredith (Tek Art) p143.
Cover design by Tony Richardson, Wooden Ark Ltd.
Cover photograph courtesy of Getty Images/Anna Bryukhanova.

Picture research by Susannah Jayes.

The authors would like to thank the schools, teachers and students whose input has been invaluable in preparing this new edition. They would also like to thank the editorial and design teams at Macmillan for doing such a great job of organizing the material and bringing it to life.

The publishers would like to thank the following educators who reviewed materials and provided us with invaluable insight and feedback for the development of *masterMind* 2nd edition:

Isidro Almedarez, Deniz Atesok, Monica Delgadillo, Elaine Hodgson, Mark Lloyd, Rufus Vaughan-Spruce, Kristof van Houdt, Rob Duncan, James Conboy, Jonathan Danby, Fiona Craig, Martin Guilfoyle, Rodrigo Rosa.

The authors and publishers would like to thank the following for permission to reproduce material:

Biographical material from www.pinksmith.com/bio.php. Used with permission. Extract from 'The Vital Role of Play in Early Childhood Education' originally published on the website of the International Association for Steiner Waldorf Early Childhood Education, www.iaswece.org. Written by Joan Almon, former chair of the Waldorf Early Childhood Association of North America and co-founder of the Alliance for Childhood. Used with permission. Material adapted from Information from http://www.obesitypanacea.com/ by Travis Saunders and Peter Janiszewski. Used with Permission. Excerpt from 'River Town: Two Years on the Yangtze' by Peter Hessler. © Peter Hessler 2001. Published by Harper Collins. Printed with permission.

The authors and publishers would like to thank the following for permission to reproduce their photographs:

Alamy/Alis Photo p103, Alamy/Christopher Bailey p128,Alamy/DBURKE p158(tl), Alamy/canadbrian p81(tr), Alamy/Cleaview (Hand) p117(tr), Alamy/Alistair Cotton p116(cm), Alamy/Nik Goulthorp p81(cr), Alamy/John Henshall p118(br), Alamy/Horizons WWP p141(tr), Alamy/D.Hurst p89, Alamy/imageBROKER p162(tr), Alamy/Stephen Lloyd Spain p99, Alamy/Mode Images p87, Alamy/ Luc Novovitch p86(cr), Alamy/Dale O'Dell pp116, 117(cl), Alamy/David O'Shea p135, Alamy/ Photodreams1 p129, Alamy/Pictorial Press Ltd p119, Alamy/ Puschmann p92(cl), Alamy/James Quine p83, Alamy/Ivelin Radkov p122, Alamy/John Robertson p117(cr), Alamy/Science Photo Library p118(2), Alamy/ Shotshop GmbH p136, Alamy/Jan Sochor p141(bcl), Alamy/Christopher Stewart p127(t), Alamy/Tetra Images pp112(cl), 161, Alamy/ Kristoffer Tripplaar p158(tl), Alamy/Zoonar GmbH p140(cr); **Bridgeman Images**/ Aboriginal painting, art gallery, Alice Springs, Australia / De Agostini Picture Library / G. Sioen p93(tl), Bridgeman Images/Ayusco 2 am, 1987 (oil on canvas), Carrington, Leonora (1917-2011) / The Israel Museum, Jerusalem, Israel /Vera & Arturo Schwarz Collection of Dada and Surrealist Art © ARS, NY and DACS, London 2014 pp94(tr), 159(cm), Bridgeman Images/ Contra-Composition of Dissonances, XVI, 1925, Doesburg, Theo van (1883-1931) / Haags Gemeentemuseum, The Hague, Netherlands p93(bl), Bridgeman Images/ Girl with a Pearl Earring, c.1665-6 (oil on canvas), Vermeer, Jan (Johannes) (1632-75) / Mauritshuis, The Hague, The Netherlands pp93(cr), 159(tc), Bridgeman Images/Man with a Guitar, 1914 (oil on canvas), Braque, Georges (1882-1963) / Musee National d'Art Moderne, Centre Pompidou, Paris, France / Giraudon © ADAGP, Paris and DACS, London 2014 p93(cl), Bridgeman Images/ Mirror Lake, Yosemite Valley, USA, 1861-75 (b/w photo), Watkins, Carleton Emmons (1829-1916) / © Royal Geographical Society, London, UK pp93(br), 159(tr), Bridgeman Images/ Scenes of Hermits' Long Days in the Quiet Mountains (ink and colour on silk), Yin, Tang (1470-1523) / Private Collection / Photo © Christie's Images p93(cm), Bridgeman Images/ The Persistence of Memory, 1931 (oil on canvas), Dali, Salvador (1904-89) / Museum of Modern Art, New York, USA/ Salvador Dali, Fundació Gala-Salvador Dalí, DACS, 2014 p94(tm); **Corbis**/2/Mel Yates/ Ocean/ Corbis p107 (cr), Corbis/68/ George Doyle/Ocean p137, Corbis/Bettmann pp129 (tr), 154, Corbis/145/ Bill Boch/Ocean p81(cl), Corbis/Burstein Collection © 2014 Maryland College Institute of Art (MICA), Rights Administered by ARS, NY and DACS, London, All Rights Reserved pp95, 159(tcr), Corbis/Dean Conger p141(tcl), Corbis/Yury Goldenshtein/Demotix p117(br), Corbis/JGI/Jamie Grill/Blend Images p88(cml), Corbis/Lawrence Manning p157(tr), Corbis/Maskot p109, Corbis/Jean-Paul Pelissier/Reuters p139(tr), Corbis/Holger Spiering/Westend61 p105 (tcr), Corbis/ Granger Wootz/Blend Images p112(cr); **Jean-Luc Cornec**/ TribuT (1995/2014) © DACS 2014 p92; **Getty Images**/apomares p124, Getty Images/Walter Bibikow p146(cl), Getty Image/Blend Images – Jade p108, Getty Images/Buena Vista Images p128(cr), Getty Images/ Burke/Triolo Productions p152(tl), Getty Images/ Gary Clark/Contributor p131, Getty Images/Neale Clarke p144, Getty Images/De Agostini Picture Library p129(cr), Getty Images/Epokydude p82, Getty Images/ Fuse p81(tl), Getty Images/Guenter Guni p141(tl), Getty Images/Johnny Haglund p141(br), Getty Images/Paul Harizan p88(cr), Getty Images/Hero Images pp106, 148, Getty Images/Mike Hill p162(tl), Getty Images/Jupiterimages p86(tr), Getty Images/Kidstock p105(tcl) Getty Images/MKucova p104, Getty Images/G. Brad Lewis p140, Getty Images/JOHN MACDOUGALL/AFP p97, Getty Images/ Mondadori via Getty Images p129(bl), Getty Images/ Mother Image/Royalty Free/mother image/Fuse p132, Getty Images/MACIEJ NOSKOWSKI p120, Getty Images/Richard Nebesky p81(br), Getty Images/Michael Ochs Archives/ Stringer p133, Getty Images/OJO Imagesp107(br), Getty Images/Jose Luis Pelaez p88(cm), Getty Images/Pgiam p125, Getty Images/Redferns via Getty Images p130, Getty Images/Alberto E.Rodriguez/Staff p129(tl), Getty Images/ROBERTO SCHMIDT/AFP p141(bl), Getty Images/The Asahi Shimbun Premium/Contributor p141(br), Getty Images/STOCK4B Creative p110, Getty Images/Tetra Images p134, Getty Images/TommL p151, Getty Images/Benjamin Torode p100, Getty Images/Betsie Van Der Meer p123, Getty Images/Brad Wilson p104(cr); **Lady Pink** p98; **PhotoDisc**/Getty Images (Cat) p117(tr); **Photoshot**/TIPS p117(tl); **Rex Features** p117(bl), Rex Features/Amos Chapple p141 (tcr), Rex Features/ CHINA SPAN Keren SU / Sunset p146(b), Rex Features/David Fisher p129(br); **Superstock**/Blend Images p88(cl); **Story of Stuff**/www.storyofstuff.com p84; **Thinkstock**/KatarzynaBialasiewicz p118(3), Thinkstock/Digital Vision p88(tcmr), Thinkstock/Dorling Kindersley p145, Thinkstock/Fuse p105(cl), Thinkstock/hroe p80, Thinkstock/luxizeng p118(1), Thinkstock/simonekesh p80 (cr), Thinkstock/ Milacroft p115, Thinkstock/omgimages p88(tr), Thinkstock/pxhidalgo p162(tm), Thinkstock/sprokop p142, Thinkstock/ Thermchai p158(tc), Thinkstock/Mike Watson Images p105(cr), Thinkstock/Lisa F. Young p105(br); **Trinh Tuan**, Vietnam pp96, 159 (cl).

Printed and bound in Thailand.

2018 2017 2016 2015
10 9 8 7 6 5 4 3 2 1